Colin (s

LIFE IN ANECDOTES

A Life in Anecdotes was written from memories and, whilst true and correct to the best of the author's knowledge, should any matter aggrieve anybody he would offer his sincere apologies.

Copyright © Colin Groves 2010

Colin Groves asserts the moral right to be identified as the author of this work.

ISBN 978-0-9544299-9-7

Published by Hanover Books
www.hanoverbooks.co.uk

H

All rights reserved. No part of this publication may be reproduced, stored in a retrieval system, or transmitted, in any form or by any means, electronic, mechanical, photocopying, recording or otherwise, without the prior permission of the publishers.

Dedication

I dedicate this book to my grandchildren:

Jack and Holly,
Fred and Connie
Joe and Charlie

Acknowledgement

I gratefully acknowledge the forbearance shown by my wife, Jane, to my post marital projects.

Contents

Chapter 1 – Antecedents 1
Chapter 2 – Early Days 28
Chapter 3 – Teens 47
Chapter 4 – National Service and Hadens 72
Chapter 5 – Consulting 117
Chapter 6 – Influences 144
Chapter 7 – Family and Other Matters 160
Chapter 8 – Dogs 187
Chapter 9 – Boats 197
Chapter 10 – Cars and Bikes Part 1 244
Chapter 11 – Cars and Bikes Part 2 264
Chapter 12 – Cars and Bikes Part 3 284
Chapter 13 – Cars and Bikes in Retirement 302

List of Photographs

Colin Groves – Oil Portrait by Harold Streeter 1949
Frontispiece
1. Grove House 126
2. Bathrad Leaflet 139
3. Severals House... 178
4. Runt 208
5. Sevorg.. 211
6. McFly – Top level yacht racing 230
7. Upshot... 233
8. Upshot off Tahiti 235
9. Grampus – Steam Launch 239
10 Sixty-six ft motor yacht 240
11. Austin 750 Formula Car 1953 265
12. Karmann Ghia 288
13. Austin 7 Tourer.. 307
14. Rexette – Jane up.. 310
15. Fiat 501S racer 317
16. Austin Seven Special 319
17. De Dion Bouton 322
18. Fiat 501 Tourer 327

Foreword

I bet that before reading this none of my grandchildren knew that through a few generations back they are descended from the British Boxing Champion. In fact, I am conscious that my grandchildren and to some extent my children have very little knowledge of their forefathers.

This is a great pity. There is no sense of continuity for the family – no sense of family history.

This lack of knowledge is in no way their fault. It comes about because the last two or three generations have been caught up in the modern frenetic way of life where family history is not on any agenda.

To try and address this omission I have recorded in this book a few anecdotes about myself. This is most definitely not an ego trip for me nor is it my autobiography.

By definition anecdotes are personal and therefore I include other people only when they impact directly on the story.

Hopefully after reading this book my grandchildren will be able to carry forward some family history which they can augment by enquiries of others of previous generations.

My grandchildren will probably still think of me as an "old fart" but perhaps they will not want to add the prefix "boring".

Colin Groves,
January 2010

Chapter 1 - Antecedents

My father was Frederick Groves born 22nd January 1899 died 4th December 1978, my mother was Rose Isabel Groves (nee Ward) born 7th March 1904 died 24th January 1966.

I was born on the 3rd February 1931 at Whipps Cross Hospital, London E17. It was a difficult birth which resulted in my mother having a hysterectomy. I was reminded periodically that I was the cause of my mother's inability to have further children and this particularly affected my lifelong relationship with my adopted sister Beverley.

As I grew up I was able to piece together some information about my grandparents and in one case my great, great grandfather.

My mother was the middle of three sisters the eldest was Lilly, known as Silly Lilly and the youngest was Kitty. These girls had a much older brother Bert.

On my fathers side, for most of my early life I thought he was an only child but discovered later that he had an elder brother who had been a motorcycle dispatch rider in the First World War (1914-1918) and had been wounded and suffered incurable brain damage which kept him in a mental hospital at Goodmayes in Essex from

Chapter 1

which he was never discharged. He died in the 1950s.

His existence was never mentioned and I only knew of him after my grandfather died, when the duty of visits to Goodmayes, previously exclusively my grandfather's, fell to my father.

I know nothing about my father's brother not even his name. This may be considered odd today but back in the 1930s the social stigma attached to mental problems whether by illness or accident meant that such things were kept very quiet and never mentioned.

My paternal grandfather was a very cold, unbending, private man whom I never really got to know. I think of him as typical of a stuffy Victorian. Even when he was old and ill and living with us to avoid the bombing in World War II we never saw him other than washed, shaved and what he considered properly dressed in a stiff detachable collar and tie and waistcoat with watch chain, etc.

He did not seem to acknowledge either my or my sisters existence.

My paternal grandmother was a tiny woman who always wore the clothes of her youth, high-necked white blouses and long black skirt. I remember her as sweet and kind and a giver of boiled sweets from a tin in her kitchen. She died when I was about six years old.

In later years I found there was more to my father's father than I realised. He and my grandmother were childhood sweethearts who vowed to marry. My grandfather was apprentice to and became a coachbuilder, that is wooden horse drawn coaches. Although a highly skilled trade it did not pay young men very much money. Just after finishing his apprenticeship at about eighteen years old there was news of a gold find in Australia. My grandfather asked his sweetheart to wait for him and took ship, at steerage fare, to Australia to look for gold. He found some but instead of getting gold fever, when he had enough gold to marry his girl and set up home he left Australia and did exactly that. A demonstration of Victorian standards and discipline, which I think remarkable. I came to know this because on his watch chain, which he always wore, there dangled what I had thought was a piece of opaque glass. When he died I looked at this charm to find it was quartz rock with a thread of gold in it. My father told me that this was a memento of his father's gold prospecting and was a tiny thread of real gold. What happened to that I do not know. All that I know my father inherited were some of my grandfather's tools. My father did not know how to use these tools and they gradually got broken and lost although I still have a few stored in my workshop.

The one lasting memory I have of my paternal grandfather was his house in Leytonstone, the one he bought on return from Australia. My grandfather plied the trade of coachbuilder his

Chapter 1

whole working life and applied his skills to his house. As a child I remember being fascinated by the fact that you could not slam any door or any drawer in the house because he had fitted everything so well that the air pressure generated in shutting a door or drawer had to seep out slowly. I still have one of my grandfather's apprentice pieces, a chest of twelve small drawers still sound after over a hundred years of use.

In contrast my maternal grandfather, known as Buba, was a very colourful and open character with whom I had a close relationship. Buba was an impressive man over six feet tall, bald and very well built and showing little visual evidence of being a professional boxer other than a slightly broken nose. I asked him how he managed not to look like old boxers generally did, he replied it was due to the length of his arms and his quickness on his feet.

Buba was the grandson of Jem Ward.

Jem Ward, born 26 December 1800, died 3 April 1884, was an English bare knuckle boxer. Described by contemporary press as "A fine fighter and powerfully built man" he was the English champion boxer from 1825 until 1831. However, he is most noticeable for being the first boxer to be officially disciplined for deliberately losing a fight. During his fighting career he was nicknamed "The Black Diamond" – I am not sure why as he certainly was not a negro. In his retirement he became a successful artist.

Antecedents

Jem Ward became a boxer in 1815 aged 15 years of age. He was 5ft 11 inches tall and weighed 12 stone. His first fight was victorious against George Robinson and from this point he never lost a match until he lost to Bill Abbot in 1822. This was the controversial bout that wrecked Jem Ward's early professional career. He was heard to call to his opponent "Now, Bill, look sharp, hit me and I'll go down." He was promptly hit and fell to the ground. Abbot was considered to be an inferior boxer to Jem Ward, and suspicions were immediately aroused. The Pugilistic Society, the body which then governed boxing and enforced the London Prize Ring Rules, held an inquiry. Eventually after confessing he had received a £100 bribe to lose, Jem Ward was banned from fighting in any contest governed by the Society. In this era boxing was heavily betted upon, by members of all strata of society, including the sons of King George III. The incident has left Jem Ward's reputation with a lasting stigma. Jem Ward was the elder brother of the boxer Nick Ward, who also had a reputation for using unfair tactics. Nick Ward, however, did not achieve the same success as his brother in the ring.

Deprived of his living Jem Ward was reduced to travelling the country fighting under assumed names at fairs or in any chance ungoverned brawl where he could possibly pick up a prize. Once early in 1823 when attending a bout as a

Chapter 1

spectator, he was called upon to enter the ring when the planned fight ended prematurely and someone was needed to provide entertainment to keep the crowd present and spending money. He fought Ned Baldwin and defeated him, but the match was void due to his ban. Under the pseudonym Sawney Wilson, and claiming to be an inexperienced boy, he beat the champion Joe Rickens, thus making the bookmakers a fortune.

Later, in 1823, the Pugilistic Society decided to re-allow him to enter their fights.

After his reinstatement he lost the first fight to Josh Hudson. In 1825, anxious for publicity and thus money, he challenged and fought the reigning heavyweight champion Tom Cannon. This proved to be the very high profile match Jem Ward needed, with Cannon seconded by two previous champions Tom Spring and Tom Cribb, names guaranteed to draw the crowds. The match took place on 19 July 1825 at Stanfield Park on a very hot day with the temperature reputedly over 90 degrees Fahrenheit. It took Jem Ward just over 10 minutes to dispatch Cannon and become the new English champion.

Following the victory Jem Ward led a life of ease and dissipation for two years, having bought a public house. In 1827 he was finally forced by public opinion to return to the ring, and accept a challenge from Peter Crawley. He was defeated by Crawley but quickly reclaimed the title when Crawley retired immediately after their match.

Jem Ward's last match was in 1831. On July 12 he fought his last fight against the Irish Champion, Simon Byrne. After an hour and seventeen minutes Jem Ward was victorious, and retained his heavyweight title until his retirement in 1831.

His 1831 retirement was forced. Jem Ward had received criticism for refusing to face the younger challenger, James Burke, and rather than fight he retired and relinquished his title. However, he did not relinquish to Burke his championship belt, when pressed he agreed to hand it over to the victor of Burke's match against his last adversary Simon Byrne in 1833. However, Jem Ward refused to hand over the belt when Burke beat Byrne whom Jem Ward supported. Byrne, who had been knocked unconscious died three days after the fight, Burke was tried and acquitted of his murder but Jem Ward still refused to part with the championship belt. He finally handed the belt over to William 'Bendigo' Thompson at the Queen's Theatre in Liverpool following the latter's defeat of Burke in 1839.

In retirement he kept the "York Hotel" in Liverpool, where he was taught to paint by his great friend the artist William Daniels, he became an accomplished and proficient artist exhibiting his work in London and Liverpool. As a musician he played both the violin and the flute, and sang in concerts. He also taught the boxing art to students, one of whom, Tom King, went on to

Chapter 1

defeat the legendary Jem Mace to become heavyweight champion in 1863. Ward died in 1884 at his home in Liverpool. He was elected to the International Boxing Hall of Fame in 1995.

I have a very clear recollection of being taken by Buba to Waterloo Hotel, which was opposite Waterloo station in London, and there being shown on the half landing of the main twin curve staircase a larger than life oil painting of Jem Ward in that curious pose of bare fist fighters and wearing a prize belt with huge brass medallions. It transpired that the Waterloo Hotel was one of Jem Wards sponsors. Of course, Buba was very proud of his grandfather and had a large quantity of mementos and press cuttings of his career including the belt in the picture in the Waterloo Hotel.

My maternal grandmother, known as Nana, was a large bosomed fierce and very bad tempered cockney woman who used to periodically fly off into uncontrollable rages. After Buba and Nana had retired to Clacton-on-Sea they had a big row over something and after Buba had gone out for a walk to get away from it all Nana put all Jem Ward's mementos on a bonfire and burnt them. The belt medallions were saved. Buba never forgave her.

Buba followed in his grandfather's footsteps and became a professional boxer at the end of the bare fist days when the Queensberry Rules were being introduced. After a period when boxers fought with a leather strap over their knuckles, the use of padded gloves and limited rounds as we have today became compulsory.

At this stage Buba retired from boxing. As a child I asked him why when the use of padded gloves could be expected to make boxing safer. He replied that that was not the case. With bare knuckles you could not hit your opponent very hard else you hurt your hand, whereas with a padded gloved fist you could hit as hard as you liked. Further, with bare fists not being able to hit hard allowed very long fights – usually lost when one party became exhausted. Gloved fights were limited in round duration and overall length in an attempt to avoid brain damage from being hit really hard over a long period.

On retiring from boxing Buba bought a pub in the East End of London which he ran successfully so he was able to embark on other business ventures. Among these were the acquisition of an initial major shareholding in the Green Gates Cinema in, I think, East Ham London, which was by far the biggest cinema in the country. After a couple of years Buba did not think that there was any future in films and cinemas and sold his shares at a knock down price.

Buba thought that Christmas crackers were of appalling quality and gave poor value for money and that there was a market for more up-market quality Christmas crackers. Shortly after one

Chapter 1

Christmas he set up a cracker making business, took on staff and made a quantity of crackers as fast as he could. He promptly ran into the problem of stock storage. Boxes of a dozen crackers have a large volume. To overcome this difficulty Buba rented a range of railway arches for storage and then spent the next ten or eleven months producing and storing crackers. Come the next Christmas Buba started distributing these crackers to up-market stores only to immediately have crackers returned and orders cancelled because the crackers did not crack. The railway arches were damp, which had ruined every cracker. Buba lost a lot of money and closed down the cracker business.

After some years Buba bought a large pub called the Royal Oak in Highams Park, Woodford Green in Essex only some half mile from where I lived as a child. He ran this pub with his son Bert.

I have many memories of my visits to this pub during my early childhood where I was often left when my parents had to go somewhere and didn't want to take me. As a ritual my parents used to walk me and latterly my sister down to the pub on Sunday mornings. My parents and sister went upstairs with my grandmother but I used to stay in the bar with Buba. He used to sit me on the high counter in the Saloon bar and give me one of the huge arrowroot biscuits, which were kept in a glass jar with a battered aluminium lid. The biscuits were very dry and designed to give people a thirst, not appealing to a child to eat. I used to chew it up and blow out a spray of crumbs. Great sport but if my grandmother had caught me I would have been in deep trouble.

Beer was delivered to the pub by brewer's dray pulled by two shire horses and manned by two big chaps in leather aprons. The breweries were very proud of their drays and horses and these were kept in immaculate order, very smart and shiny. The cellar was accessed by two hinged steel doors in the pavement through which barrels slid down on a sort of wooden ladder with bent steel rungs to fit the barrel shape. During deliveries a drayman would feed the horses with nosebags of oats and afterwards go into the pub for a pint or two of beer. Buba used to stand beside the dray and supervise the offloading and when I was there he would lift me onto the back of one of the horses just behind its neck where the position of the harness would allow. There I would sit only to be lifted down when the horses had finished eating their oats and the drayman returned to set off back to their depot. I remember very well the feel of the warm shiny horse's coat on my legs which stuck out sideways because of the width of the horse's back. I was quite used to the horses throwing up their heads to get the last of the oats in the bottom of the bag but on one occasion I was not paying attention and the horse threw up its head when I was not expecting it and I remember to this day, more than seventy years later, the

Chapter 1

impact of the horses neck and mane on my face. I was dazed and my nose bled copiously. Buba rushed me indoors and eventually stemmed the flow of blood. Nana made a hell of a fuss about blood on the floor but not a word of sympathy for me. She forbade me to ever sit on a brewery horse again. A restriction, which Buba and I ignored thereafter.

I think that blow on my nose as a child was the cause of my never growing a bone in my nose. From the bridge to the tip of my nose has always been flexible as if the normal bone has been replaced by cartilage. This is a very useful feature – there have been at least five occasions when I have injured my nose to the extent that it would certainly have been broken if it had contained a normal bone. These events merely bruised my nose with no lasting effects.

Buba must have had a part-time interest in teaching or organizing boxing with the Metropolitan Police because I have a clear memory of being taken to, I think, Hendon Police College, for their summer open day which included, presumably, the final of some southern area police amateur boxing competition. Midway through the programme of bouts Buba appeared in the ring in white trousers and polo necked sweater with boxing gloves on and proceeded to fight an exhibition bout simultaneously with four large policemen in black singlets and shorts. All in fun of course but mighty impressive for a small grandson.

On another occasion when I was in the Royal Oak pub eating my arrowroot biscuits in the saloon bar there was a commotion in the public bar which I could see into from where I was. There were two guardsmen, this was pre-war and these chaps were regular soldiers very rough and tough characters. I was told afterwards they had been drinking since opening time and were drunk and spoiling for a fight. I saw Buba who must have been over sixty years old give a nod to uncle Bert who was behind the bar serving as well, Buba then put a hand on the high bar, vaulted over, landed behind one of the guardsman, grabbed him by the seat of his trousers and the collar of his uniform and virtually lifting him off the ground propelled him to the street door and threw him out down the flight of steps at that end of the pub. Uncle Bert did exactly the same thing with the other guardsman, so obviously it was a rehearsed method of dealing with troublemakers. The guardsmen did not reappear. The whole smooth operation without a word being spoken was most impressive to a small boy.

A couple more memories of Buba are after he and Nana retired to Clacton on Sea in Essex in the late nineteen thirties. Buba was always immaculately dressed in a pearl grey suit with a waistcoat and hat – in winter a bowler and in summer a straw boater. These boaters he bought

Chapter 1

in half dozen lots from some hatter in London. When I was down in Clacton visiting, which seemed to be frequently, Buba and I would go out for walks down to the town and along the seafront with me at full upwards stretch holding his hand. In those days in sunny weather most shops had a sunblind which they pulled down and out on hinged steel arms over the pavement to shield the front of the shop. These blinds were designed to provide just enough head room for the average person. This was not enough for Buba who would frequently walk into them and the top of his straw boater would be broken off and stand up. Buba would then let rip with a string of swear words which he could keep up for what seemed like ten minutes without repeating himself. He would then apologise to me and we would go back home and get a replacement boater from his hatbox before we set out again.

As a young lad Buba had worked briefly in a printing works where he lost the top one of his fingers in a machine. The finger healed and he was left with the beginning of the original fingernail, which then became a round horn nail, which grew at the normal rate, and this needed periodic cutting. On his watch chain Buba had a small pearl handled penknife. On occasion Buba would be sitting in his chair reading his paper when he would notice that this horn nail was getting long and needed trimming. No doubt this horn nail was beyond the capabilities of normal nail clippers because Buba would open up his little penknife, lay the offending finger on his paper on the arm of his chair, take one sighting with the knife blade and then bring it down smartly to chop off the end of the nail which flew off into the distance. My inspection of the finger afterwards revealed the nail was chopped off precisely flush with the end of his finger. Seventy or so years of practice I suppose but nevertheless impressive I thought.

I have mentioned that Uncle Bert, who like his father did a bit of boxing in his young days, retired, married my aunt Hilda, started a family and went to work with his father in the pubs, ending up in the Royal Oak. When I knew him he was a younger version of his father, more heavily built and only six feet or so tall. When Buba retired he must have sold the Royal Oak for a goodly sum which he shared with Bert. Bert did not retire but moved to Clacton where his parents were and embarked on a series of business ventures with most of which he had the luck of the devil and was successful by no effort on his part.

When Bert moved to Clacton in the late 1930s cars were becoming more common and Bert thought he would like to get into the car business by buying a garage. In those days the Clacton Town Council developed the promenade with gardens behind but ran out of money and just

Chapter 1

stopped at a hedge with a rough field beyond. There was a gate in the hedge inside which there was a tatty corrugated iron building which had a sign outside saying Garage. There were no petrol pumps, no proper workshop and the building was surrounded by rusting engines overgrown with brambles. It was this 'garage' that Bert bought. He subsequently discovered that the garage seldom took in any car work, what it survived on was repairing the boat engines from the Clacton beach inshore fishing fleet which used old car engines in their boats.

Bert knew no engineering and left running the Garage to the three men who had worked there before he bought it. Bert spent most days there playing at being boss and looking after the finances.

He had only owned the garage for a few months when two men in bowler hats, black jackets and striped trousers, business wear of the period, came in and said they would like to buy the garage at a price a good deal more than Bert had paid for it. Most people would have jumped at a quick profit but Bert was a canny man and said "No, he did not want to sell his livelihood". The men went away, only to return a few weeks later with an offer which was some twice what Bert had paid and when that was refused they returned again after another few weeks with an even higher offer which Bert also turned down, sensing there was more to this affair than was obvious. A short time after this last visit contractors arrived and started developing the field to become Butlins Holiday Camp in Clacton. This was completed in quick time and opened with Bert's tatty little garage building just inside the main gate.

An attraction to the holiday makers of the Clacton Butlins was the free use of side by side pedal-powered four wheeled bikes for transport into the town centre, which was some distance away. The rate of damage to these pedal cycles was high and all of the repair business naturally came to the workshop on the site, Bert's garage. During the first year of Butlins operation Bert made a small fortune repairing these peddle cycles at any rate he chose to charge. During the first winter after Butlins opened the two suited men with briefcases turned up again and said to Bert "You can see now why we wanted this garage site – and we cannot have this unsuitable building in our camp so name a price at which you will sell".

The family never knew how much Bert sold the garage for but it was a lot of money.

With the proceeds from the garage sale Bert decided that he would be a gentleman farmer and bought a virtually useless farm just outside Clacton behind the sea wall with land that was very salty and covered with flints up to the size of a football. Bert rented out all the land to adjoining subsistence farmers, commissioned a navel architect to design a motor yacht, and engaged

Chapter 1

local boat builders to build the yacht onto a giant trolley made from an old lorry chassis, all in the barn on the farm. I remember seeing this boat in the barn nearing completion it looked huge. It was probably about fifty feet in overall length.

The boat was completed but not launched at the beginning of World War II. Sometime after this one of Bert's friends telephoned to warn him that the police were commandeering boats for the war effort and they knew of his boat. Bert was not going to give up his new boat so at the dead of night he and some chums towed the boat with a tractor to marshland near Brightlingsea a few miles from Clacton and there launched the boat in a largely hidden creek, then they sheeted the boat up to protect and conceal it. Sure enough the police called and Bert showed them the empty barn and denied having a boat. He and his chums congratulated themselves on being very clever until it transpired the boats collected were the Dunkirk little ships which got British troops off the beaches at Dunkirk, this event became a National Victory with boats and their crews being honoured. The shame and social stigma for not sending your boat to Dunkirk would have been too much for Bert, the boat had to stay hidden. It became a ritual for Bert and some of the family to drive out about once a month in their Austin 12-4 heavy car on fine Sundays to check on the boat from the road some two hundred yards away from its location. About a year after Dunkirk they went out one Sunday and the boat was gone, they did not know whether it had been stolen or broken adrift and gone out to sea or lost when it had been attacked and sunk by German aircraft which were over the East coast all the time at that stage of the War. Bert could not speak to the authorities so never knew what happened to his boat.

As a 'gentleman' farmer Bert was invited to a local dignitaries pheasant shoot. He asked what he should wear and was told the correct apparel and advised he had to get a pair of double barrel shotguns. Bert had none of this stuff so he went up to the St James area of the west end of London to get kitted out. He went to a Saville Row tailor who duly measured him for a shooting suit and told him he would need two fittings and the suit would be ready in about six months. "No," said Bert "I have to wear it this weekend." The tailor said "We don't do ready to wear garments," but when Bert grumbled said they had a suit which would roughly fit Bert made for someone who had been killed in the War. Bert bought that. The tailor said he would need shooting boots and directed him to a top boot maker. Here again the bespoke handmade boots were on a long delivery but Bert was able to buy boots which were made for somebody who had been killed, this time though the boots were about four sizes too large but Bert had them anyway. Finally he was directed to Purdey's a famous gunsmiths. Yet again these guns were made to fit their owner, a

Chapter 1

long process, Bert asked for any made for someone who had died, and when they had he bought a pair of matched Purdey 12 bore shotguns.

Come the Saturday of the shoot, Bert in his finery and with his guns turned up at the shoot. After a few whiskies he was introduced to his loader for the day and taken to his butt, a sort of small enclosure, where you and your loader stood while the local peasantry drove pheasants into the air and towards you. Bert banged away without hitting anything for the first drive. When that was finished there was a period of waiting. The loader asked Bert to give him the loaded gun he was holding. "No," said Bert, now full of confidence and he put the gun muzzle down on his foot out of the mud and leant his elbow on the shoulder part for a rest. The gun went off. By sheer good luck the muzzle was resting on the oversized toe of the too- large-for-Bert-boots. He lost the end of his big toe. After Bert had come out of hospital he had had enough of shooting and would never go again.

As the War progressed the German pilots were becoming younger and more nervous and when crossing the East coast on the way to London they saw Bert's farm isolated and undefended and they would aimlessly shoot up the area and drop a small bomb or two so they could go home safely with their magazines empty and thus complete their missions. This became a nuisance to Bert and his family so he rented a house further inland

Antecedents

and bought an old lorry and moved the family and some of the furniture to this house which was at the end of a terrace of farm labourers' cottages beside which there was a small field. Bert had no right to use the field but after offloading he parked the lorry there to be out of the narrow lane.

That first evening there was a knock at the door and there was a chap who had seen the lorry and was asking Bert if he could do a removal job for him. Always with his eye to business Bert said yes he would do the job the following day. This led to other jobs, so Bert became a haulage company, which gave him access to rationed petrol and diesel. He bought other lorries at knockdown prices and took on local men as drivers. By the end of the War he had twelve lorries and drivers, which were always busy and Bert made a lot of money. Sometime after the War road transport was nationalized. The Government bought Bert out for a very large sum on which he retired never to work again.

When Bert and the family were moving out of the farm one son, Graham, had wanted to take his goldfish, kept in a tank in his bedroom. The lorry was already fully loaded with no space for a fish tank so Bert refused but, to save the goldfish from starvation, emptied the tank into the large pond in the middle of the farmyard.

After the family returned to the farm at the end of the war in Europe Bert saw in the newspaper that Gamages, a department store in London,

Chapter 1

which before the war made a speciality of providing goldfish, were wanting goldfish for sale as the traditional source, Japan, was still at war. At the same time Bert found that the pond in the farmyard was alive with goldfish – descendants of the goldfish put in the pond when leaving the farm a couple of years before. Bert put a large water tank on the back of one of his lorries, bought a lot of children's fishing nets on cane handles and put a notice at the farm gate saying "One penny for each goldfish caught – nets supplied". Children came from miles around, including my cousins David and Dick and I, to catch goldfish which everyone did so that after some days the pond was less well stocked. Bert suspended fishing. The fish caught were put in the tank on the lorry and were taken to Gamages where Bert sold them for, I think, six pence per inch in length: a handsome profit.

Bert decided to reduce the water level in the pond to concentrate the remaining fish. This posed a problem as the pond had no outlet. Bert solved this by inviting the local volunteer Fire Brigade, set up during the war and now meeting as a club on Wednesday nights, to bring their mobile pump and draw water from the pond to serve hoses which were used for practice on the fields surrounding the farm. This worked well and after two fire brigade sessions with children catching goldfish between, the pond was almost drained. Bert stopped further fishing leaving some twenty or so fish in the remainder of the pond to breed as the pond refilled to yield another harvest the following summer.

The pond did refill but the goldfish numbers did not increase significantly. Then Bert decided to get expert advice and brought in a fish expert. I remember the pond having a lot of unusual weed which had close layers of four or five small leaves, so that it looked like a long spring in the water. This weed lay about dried up and dead on the mud bank sides when the pond was drained. The fish expert said that he had never seen this weed outside of Japan and could not explain how it had got into the farm pond. This weed was the favourite food of goldfish and its original presence explained the copious breeding of the fish. However, children wading around in the pond and draining the water had caused all the weed to dry up and die and this had finished the goldfish rush which now could not be repeated. Nevertheless Bert had made a small fortune with his goldfish.

My mother's elder sister, Lilly, married a marine engineer, Richard Dixey who was appointed Superintendent of the Falmouth docks at the beginning of the War. Falmouth was the first safe haven for merchant ships damaged on the Atlantic convoys, quick repair of those ships was critically vital to Britain's survival. The country depended on food and supplies from the USA to avoid being starved into submission. So Uncle Dick had a vital role to play. He did this by

Chapter 1

working in the dockyard almost twenty four hours a day seven days a week throughout the War. He slept in his office and only came home briefly to collect washing and deal with family matters. I with my mother and sister used to visit Aunt Lilly occasionally but I saw and knew very little about Uncle Dick. However, one event I do recall when I would have been about twelve years old, was being taken to see Uncle Dick in the dockyard and him taking me down into the engine rooms of some ships under repair. My recollection of him sliding down steel ladders with cotton waste in his hands deep into the dark bowels of these ships followed very gingerly by me and a strong smell of rusting steel, fuel, and bilge water is as clear to me now, sixty years later, as it was then. This memory can be brought on by the smell of rusting steel.

At the end of the War uncle Dick was in his late forties and received all sorts of accolades and an OBE for his War efforts and was appointed Superintendent of London Docks, in those days the most prestigious job in the largest and most important docks in the country. The family moved to Romford in Essex. Uncle Dick lasted in his new job for about six months before he became ill. The doctors said that you may be in your forties but you have the body and physique of a man of ninety. Your work in the War has just worn you out and there is nothing that can be done for you. Richard Dixey died a couple of months later.

His death showed me the fallacy of the much-quoted Victorian adage of my youth in that 'hard work never killed anyone' it certainly killed Dick Dixey.

Uncle Dick and Aunt Lilly had three children, two a lot older than me, a boy Kenneth but know as Bud, and a daughter Daphne. I did not get on with either of them. Ken became a marine engineer specializing in corrosion control, I believe he died in the 1980s. His sister Daphne married a prison officer and she also died some time ago. Their third child John was a couple of years younger than me and he emigrated to the USA when he was about eighteen, I think to avoid national service. As far as I know he never returned.

My mother's younger sister Kit was a large jolly woman whom I liked a lot. She was married to Len Jackman who was a butcher with a shop at Headstone Lane near Harrow. They had three children. David who was about a year older than me, Dick who was about a year younger than me and Bob who was about four or so years younger than Dick and so was regarded by all of us as a baby. As a family we saw a good deal of the Jackmans and I, in effect, grew up with my cousins.

In the latter part of the War when German V2 rockets started the Jackmans had a close shave when a rocket exploded in the next street to their

Chapter 1

house and this experience persuaded them to move to Clacton to be near my grandparents and Kits brother Bert and away from the bombs and rockets of the London area. My mother, sister and I went to Clacton frequently and David, Dick and I had all sorts of adventures most of which involved boats of some kind, which are covered in the boats section of this book.

A notable exception was the Martello Tower in which we made our private headquarters. Martello towers were and are relatively small round forts built around the coasts, I think, in Napoleonic times, for defence. The entrance was through a small door about half way up the side so that it was about thirty feet above the ground, originally accessed by a wooden staircase which could be swung up by a block and tackle to prevent entry by the enemy. Our Martello Tower was isolated on empty land south of Clacton near the village of Jaywick and had not been touched for many many years. The access stair had long since rotted away and there was no trace of this. The massive wooden door stood partly open.

Dave, Dick and I decided that this tower was going to be our headquarters and we had to get into it. There was no way we could climb this smooth plain face so we made a sort of grapnel out of big meat hooks from Uncle Len's butcher shop, attached to lengths of stout clothes line and spent the best part of a school summer holiday throwing this arrangement up into the door opening. Eventually the grapnel hook got round the back of the partly opened door and, I think Dave, was able to climb up and pull up a rope ladder which we had made and let that down so that Dick and I could climb up. This tower was a wonderful building with walls about ten feet thick and galleries around the central core. We devised a way of pulling the ladder up from the ground with a light line, which was not very obvious from a distance. This tower then became our exclusive preserve where we played regularly until the Jackmans emigrated.

Uncle Len was not happy working for someone else after having had his own butcher's shop in Headstone Lane and never really settled in Clacton. After the War the Australian Government was very anxious to attract immigrants from the UK and offered passage to Australia for ten pounds per person. Uncle Len, Auntie Kit, Dave, Dick and baby Bob went out to Australia on this scheme in the late 1940s. My parents heard from them occasionally. After a rough start they made a life for themselves. Cousin Dick came to visit this country in the early eighties and was just as I remembered him. However he brought his very Australian wife with him and I did not like her very much.

Chapter 2 – Early Days

My father had volunteered for military service late in World War I when he was under age at seventeen. Due to the horrendous loss of lives during that war the army was desperate for recruits and, in spite of his age, accepted my father but only for non-combative duties. My father became an orderly in the army venereal disease hospital in England. He never went to France. My father's sheltered upbringing had done nothing to prepare him for this hospital full of men dying hideous deaths from syphilis. There was no cure for venereal disease in the early 1900s. This experience scarred my father for life. He had an absolutely rigid and inflexible attitude to sexual relationships outside marriage.

After the Army had finished with my father at the end of the War he was very fortunate to join what was then the London, Brighton and South Coast Railway, which was to become the Southern Railway, by being sponsored by some remote relative who was a big investor in that railway. Who this benefactor was and what became of him I never knew.

My father was a clerk in the head offices at London Waterloo station and he remained working as a clerk for the railway for his entire working life ending up as Chief Clerk to British Rail Southern Region.

My father went to Cann Hall Road School in Leytonstone, East London where he became a good footballer. After leaving school he joined the school Old Boys team which was quite big in the area. He carried on playing for this team until he married my mother. In this team he met his best friend Pat Harris, a very neat and dapper man in 1920s style who worked for Nelsons, the book publishers, who I knew in my childhood because in addition to regular visits to our house he gave me Nelson published adult books for birthdays and Christmases before I could read. I still have a number of these books.

Pat Harris died suddenly when I was about six or seven of I think kidney failure. This was my first experience of someone I knew dying; I was stunned and had great difficulty coming to terms with his death.

After giving up football on his marriage my father and mother joined a tennis club at Snakes Lane, Woodford. This was very much a family club which we seemed to go to every weekend in the Summer, my father playing most of the time while my mother made teas in the pavilion, my sister lay in her pram and I just played around sometimes with any other boys there or on my own excavating dens in enormous heaps of grass cuttings.

Chapter 2

My mother and father made many friends at the tennis club, the most significant of these were Spud and Elsie Danzey who lived at 27 Litchfield Road, Woodford about one mile from our home. They were a very nice couple, slightly younger than my parents, who became life long friends of whom we saw a great deal both in the summer at the club and in winter in each other's homes. Spud particularly was always kind and friendly toward me and it was obvious even to me as a child that Spud and Elsie wanted a family, but they remained childless until late in the War when they had a son Roger.

When he was about four years old Roger went downstairs in his dressing gown one morning to be with his father who was making porridge for breakfast. He attempted to climb up on the kitchen chair beside the cooker but stepped into the front of his dressing gown, lost his balance and in falling grabbed the handle of the saucepan of boiling water for porridge and spilt the boiling water all down his front. He died of these burns. His parents were mortified especially Spud who blamed himself for the accident. This was the first and possibly only time that I ever witnessed deep soul searching grief. Spud and Elsie went on in later years to have two further children Richard and a girl whose name I cannot now remember.

We lived in a house my parents had named Cheslyn in Oak Hill Road, Woodford Green, Essex, which they bought, newly built by a developer when they got married. This was a nice three-bedroom semi detached house at the end of a terrace of five houses. It had a fair sized front garden and a large rear garden, quite up market for the suburbs in the 1930s.

My memory of my earliest years are that it was always sunny and I spent all my time playing in the back garden wearing very short shorts and a sun hat.

Next door lived a boy of about my age, about two years, with whom I was not allowed to make contact after I caught him chopping up a large earthworm with a child's beach spade and I did not think this was a good thing, so I took the spade from him and hit him on the head with it. I recall a little shouting and some blood. I do not think he cut up any more earthworms after that.

This period, the early to mid thirties spawned a lot of odd theories for of bringing up children. With my parents I was invited to, I think, the four-year-old birthday party of the son of some tennis club friends of my parents. These people followed some weird child behaviorist's teachings that children should not be stopped from doing anything but should be allowed to find out what to do and what not to do by themselves. The party was held in the garden of a house similar to ours. In the excitement the boy went upstairs and appeared at a first floor bedroom window and called something to his mother, she replied to the

Chapter 2

effect of "do what you want". He then stepped out of the window fell to the ground and broke both legs. This resulted in an abrupt end to the party and an equally abrupt end to the family following those particular behaviourist's teachings.

In June/July 1938 when I was seven my parents adopted a new born baby girl, my sister Beverley Ann. I do not recall having any strong feelings about this at the time. I took it as being quite normal to have a new born baby girl to join the family.

Shortly after coming to us my new sister developed a very serious version of whooping cough and was critically ill for some weeks. In those days before antibiotics there appeared to be no treatment other than one or other of my parents sitting with Bev day and night burning aromatic candles. Understandably, I got very little attention during this episode and this set a pattern for my parents' relationship with me thereafter. I should emphasise that I was not then nor have ever been jealous of my sister. But I was always puzzled by the way my parents doted on her throughout her life as they had done when she was a sick baby.

Inevitably my parents' behaviour interfered with my ever getting really close to my sister and so although we grew up in the same family, we were apart.

I grew up with a boy's interests without my parents being deeply involved. An example is that when I was about ten years old and we were living in Horsham I taught myself to swim in Horsham outdoor swimming pool. I spent all school summer holidays in the swimming pool and became such a proficient swimmer that in later years I was Collyers School swimming captain and taught many of my school contemporaries how to swim to gain points for the inter-house swimming competition and even to the extent that in my late teenage years I was engaged as a part time lifeguard at Horsham swimming pool, probably because there were no men available. I also played water polo for Horsham for several years before my National Service.

When Bev was in her teens my parents decided she should learn to swim, I offered to teach her which I would really have liked to have done but this offer was declined. My parents enrolled Bev for swimming lessons with a very expensive coach in Croydon. Bev and my mother went to these lessons by train, a journey of nearly an hour from Horsham, once a week for around a year. I do not remember Bev ever swimming even after that course.

At the age of four or five I was enrolled in an infant school, Thorpe Hall Primary School that was some three quarters of a mile away from where we lived. My mother, walked me to school in the morning, brought me home again for lunch, back again for the afternoon and then collected me after school in the afternoon. This meant some

Chapter 2

six miles a day five days a week in all weathers. In those car-less days such things were considered normal.

I can remember being very a happy at Thorpe Hall School.

When I was about five or six my father attempted to make me a football enthusiast like himself by presenting me with a complete football outfit, shirt, shorts, pair of football boots and full sized leather covered football. In the family album there is a photograph of me in this get up, looking very uncomfortable. All this not withstanding I was at an infant school with no football pitch. In fact I do not recall any football pitches in our area, there were no junior teams and none of my chums played football. So it did rather put me off football for life, although I was required to play at secondary school.

Opposite to my house was Holly Crescent a road of detached houses on one side only and in one of these lived my friend George Blow with whom I had many adventures in the wooded wasteland enclosed by the crescent. These included the joint discovery of the differences between boys and girls with the very willing assistance of an older girl called Nancy who lived next door but one to George. We had primitive three wheeled bikes, which we used to ride frequently around the area on the roads, on the pavements and through the woods in those traffic free days.

Woodford Green where we lived was on the fringe of Epping Forest. Occasionally George and I would peddle off into the forest to Highams Park Lake, which was about a mile away. This lake had boats for hire, punts and sliding seat skiffs for the young bloods, which much impressed us and initiated my life long interest in boats. We used to catch tiny fish called sticklebacks with a net on the end of a cane and these we took home in a jam jar.

I mention this as an illustration of how different things were in these pre-War days. Paedophiles as far as I am aware were unknown, the roads were virtually free of traffic and what traffic there was was very slow moving. These were truly halcyon days and not nostalgic rose tinted memories.

I lost touch with George Blow when we left Woodford Green, but heard occasionally through Spud and Elsie Danzey which ended when George was killed practicing in a racing car he had build himself at Goodwood in the early 1950s. There was something in our early childhood that made us both car-racing devotees.

My father was a life long socialist and was very politically aware. In the late 1930s he became much concerned over the rise of Hitler in Germany. This concern was reinforced when he met the parents of a boy who lived near us and with whom I played. His name was Geoffrey Geiger and his father was a member of the British

Chapter 2

Nazi Movement lead by Oswald Mosley known as the 'Black Shirts'. Father Geiger would dress up in his black shirt uniform and preach the party line at every opportunity, my father dropped the Geigers like a hot brick and I was never to play with Geoffrey again. What ultimately happened to this family after war was declared I do not know.

Brief contact with the Geiger family convinced my father that the rumours coming out of Germany at that time were true and we took in a refugee Jewish girl of about sixteen years old who had been sent alone by her parents out of Germany as they could not afford for all of them to come. She lived with us for about three months until the authorities found her a permanent foster home. I remember her as a quiet sad girl with dark hair who could speak little English. She made a deep impression on me, particularly her deep concern for her family left in Germany. It brought home to me that life in the rest of the world was not all like that which I had known.

Then in 1939, unconvinced by claims of the prime minister Neville Chamberlain, my father foresaw the outbreak of World War II so that in the spring of that year, fearful of the likelihood of bombing of London area, he arranged for my mother, my sister Bev and me to go and live with the brother of my fathers secretary, a Miss Tucker, in the remote village of Elmdon in Essex.

Getting there was a problem. Elmdon had no railway and only had a bus twice a week to the nearest town, Saffron Walden, that was about fourteen miles away. I do not know how but my father persuaded David Jenkins (about whom more later) to take us in his Morris 8. For reasons I do not know this was a very clandestine affair, Bev and I were taken from our beds in the middle of a dark and wet night and driven the fifty or so miles to Elmdon.

The Tuckers lived in and ran the general store, the only shop in the village. Mr Tucker did not do very much except run a very poor smallholding behind the shop. He was a very unfriendly, unlikable strange man who I think was mentally unstable. He kept a large pig shut up in a shed behind the shop only opening the top half of the stable door to throw scraps of food in. This was the first time I had anything to do with animals and I felt very sorry for this pig, I knew it was not being treated right. We were in Elmdon for a few months and I attended the village school, which had one teacher, one room and catered for children in the area from five to fifteen years, I remember the class amounting to about ten in number.

Much to everyone's glee Mr Tucker got his come-uppance one day. While Tucker was putting food over the lower door the pig enraged by being shut up all its life charged the door, smashed it off its hinges and broke out, trampling on Tucker in the process and breaking both his legs. Tucker was taken to hospital and I never saw him again

Chapter 2

because shortly afterwards on one lovely early autumn day most of the village gathered outside the only cottage with a radio to hear Neville Chamberlain, the Prime Minister, announce that Great Britain was at War with Germany.

This changed everything.

My father's office of the Southern Railway was evacuated from Waterloo to Deepdene House, a mansion just outside Dorking in Surrey. My father let Cheslyn and rented a bungalow in Highlands Avenue, Horsham which is about fifteen miles from Dorking.

I was eight years old when we moved to Horsham and my father was anxious for me to go to Collyers Grammar School in Horsham for which one had to pass an entrance examination. To prepare for this I was sent to a fee paying preparatory school run by Miss Beryl Munroe-Higgs and situated in the medieval buildings at the top of the Causeway in Horsham. This turned out to be a bit of a confidence trick for the backward children of the very rich. I fitted neither of these criteria but my situation was saved by a very old retired teacher who had fallen on hard times and had to work for the Munroe-Higgs and who was a very good teacher indeed. From him I gleaned enough knowledge to ultimately pass the entrance examination to Collyers.

The only things I remember clearly about this preparatory school was firstly a complete lack of discipline and being at a cricket coaching class run by an eighteen year old Collyers schoolboy who demonstrated a cover drive which hit me on the head with his bat, knocking me out. This caused a bit of panic at the Munroe-Higgs camp but once I came round it seemed to cause me no trouble at all. The Munroe-Higgs School closed shortly after I left. I do not think there is any connection. Years later my dentist 'Butcher McKee' occupied part of the buildings, the other part became and still is Horsham Museum.

While I was at Munroe-Higgs School World War II had got underway. It may seem odd but the momentous War years of 1939 to 1945 did not make a great impression on me. I suppose being a child in the soft south of England insulated me from the full horrors of the War.

However some memories of this period stand out, I remember going with my mother to Horsham station where she and other ladies made tea and sandwiches and handed these out to trains of bedraggled exhausted soldiers rescued from the beaches of Dunkirk. These trains came up from Portsmouth to Horsham on the way to London.

I recall the summer of 1940 being continuous beautiful sunny weather and the Battle of Britain raging over the Horsham area, we used to watch planes, which looked like toys, wheeling around over our heads and hear the rat-a-tat of machine

Chapter 2

guns. Planes went down streaming smoke and parachutes broke out periodically.

However, I do not recall being conscious of any danger to us or of the men dying above our heads it all seemed like an improbable film.

Even later when the allies' massed bombers assembled over Sussex, so that the air was thick with planes, it was exciting to a boy but impersonal. Perhaps it was because nobody I knew was in the forces or got killed.

There was an airplane breakers yard at Faygate near Horsham where we used to cycle to get Perspex from broken windscreens and windows which we used to make into rings and things, why, I cannot remember. Here in some of the planes there were pieces of human bodies, this although unpleasant seemed disconnected from our lives.

There were occasions when this came closer to home, as when a German plane shot up Collyers School during the school summer holidays doing damage but no injury as the school was empty.

Throughout the war we lived in the bungalow in Highlands Avenue that my father had rented when we first went to Horsham. This was second in from one end of a row of some six similar bungalows all built just before the war.

We were the first tenants of our house. The house next door to us was occupied by a husband, wife and boy a little younger than me who were very obviously of far eastern origins.

They kept themselves to themselves. Initially we thought they could not speak English although subsequently that proved not to be the case. I do not remember the boy going to school or, indeed, going out of the house other than being in the garden on his own and I think he must have been bored being at home all the time. His mother suddenly invited me round for afternoon tea, my mother said I should accept . I duly went to tea. It was not a very successful outing, the boy, whose name I do not recall, was painfully shy and hardly said a word and while his mother tried to make conversation in broken English she obviously knew of nothing which would interest a normal ten year old boy. Eventually the tea party ended without any suggestion of a repeat and I went home. An unremarkable event, except for one thing. As was the fashion of the 1930s the walls of every room in their house, like ours, had timber picture rails. In their house, in every room that I saw into, the picture rails carried beautifully made models of ships – dozens of them – warships, liners and freighters. Of course, these were the only things that interested me but the boy's mother would only let me look – not touch. When I got home I told my parents about these model ships and they thought this very strange.

We had no other contact with these people, no friendship between me and their boy materialized. One fine Saturday morning about six months after my going to tea several cars arrived outside

Chapter 2

their house and some six plain clothes police and about the same number of uniformed officers went into the house next door. It was obvious that the house was vacant – although there was some furniture left behind. The plain clothes police came to our house and questioned my mother about the people who had been next door. She was very surprised that they had moved out without her knowing and, with the police, worked out that it was two days previously. She happened to mention that I was the only person she knew of who had been into the house, so the police interviewed me.

I told them about the model ships on the picture rails. They said that they were not there now and got me to describe them as best I could. My mention of the ship models interested them greatly and one of them took copious notes. The police would not disclose what was their interest in the people next door and we never did find out. The furniture and fittings were removed from the house and the house remained empty for a couple of months until rented by a Mr and Mrs Collett and their grey kitten, which my mother named Holy Smoke which stuck. The Colletts were very nice people.

We never knew what the oriental family had been up to that caused them to do a moonlight flit and attracted the attention of the police.

Like most families we had a standard issue air raid shelter partly buried in the garden, it was called, I think, an Anderson shelter. This had very little use because it was damp inside and was eventually used to grow mushrooms. In addition we had an indoor Morrison shelter which was like a large table with very stout angle steel legs and a steel plate top with rectangular mesh sides. This shelter was designed for a family of four to sleep under and protect them in the event of a house collapsing due to a bomb blast. This we did use a fair bit, particularly toward the end of the War when Britain was under attack by V1 flying bombs known as Doodlebugs.

This Morrison shelter occupied my small bedroom where it replaced my normal bed. When in use in anger, my mother, my sister and I were underneath, but when there was no danger I slept on top whilst the rest of the family had their own bedrooms. During one of these quiet periods I contracted measles, which was treated very seriously in those days. I had to stay in bed for some six weeks, but after being off-colour for the first week or so, I did not feel unwell and became very bored so my mother took pity on me and bought me a kit to build a model wartime aeroplane called a Lysander which had distinctive dihedral wings. Such kits in those days consisted of sheets of balsa wood marked out with the shapes of the component parts to be cut out with a razor blade and then assembled from a set of drawings by glueing to form the airframe which was then skinned with a form of paper shrunk on

Chapter 2

with "dope". Power for the propeller was provided by stout elastic bands. My kit was for a plane with a wing-span of about five feet. I sat up in bed with a big sheet of cardboard on my lap and spent my recovery from measles building this aeroplane. I completed the fuselage, wings and tailplane but the complete plane was too large to assemble on my bed indoors. I was eventually allowed to get up and go into the garden to complete my plane.

I found that both the wings I had made were for the same side of the plane. The drawing showed one wing and carried a note to reverse the drawing for the other wing. This I had not done, I had built the two wings of the same hand.

There was no way the wrong hand wing could be made to work, and I had no materials left to build another wing, so something like a month's work had come to nothing. I broke up this model and have had nothing to do with models ever since, but this experience did teach me a valuable lesson – "Read the instructions before assembly".

V1 – Doodlebugs were pilot-less flying bombs with wings, propelled by a ram jet engine. They were launched from ramps in Northern France and flew very fast on a fixed course until the fuel ran out when they glided steeply to explode on contact with the ground. One of the several fixed flight courses on route to London was straight up Highlands Avenue where we lived. I recall being in the Morrison shelter hearing the V1s passing overhead every three or four minutes and there was a heart stopping moment when the engines cut out and the short wait until an almighty bang. A number of these flying bombs fell in the Horsham area mainly out in the country, but none near us.

When these flying bombs started they caught the British authorities by surprise and they had no defence against them but after a few months we had developed several means to combat them. There was an American fighter plane, the only type in service that was fast enough to keep pace with the V1. These were flown by madcap pilots who would fly alongside a V1 before it reached the British coast, get their wing under the wing of the V1 and tip it up to upset the V1s gyro and send it at least ninety degrees off course. In addition a very early form of computer called a Predictor was coupled directly to anti aircraft guns to predict the position of the V1 at a future time so the guns could be loaded, positioned and fired automatically. Because the V1s flew straight and level the success rate of these Predictor controlled guns was very high. A lot of bombs exploded harmlessly in the air.

During my national service in REME I went to the Anti Aircraft School of Instruction at Lydd in Kent where I was trained in these Predictors and their accoutrements, as they were still in current army issue in the early 1950s.

When the Germans realised that the effect of the V1 flying bombs had been diluted they

Chapter 2

introduced the V2 a much more frightening weapon. The V2 was a rocket filled with explosives fired in Northern France, aimed at London. There was no warning of these, you neither saw nor heard anything before an almighty explosion. They unnerved my Uncle Len and Aunt Kitty to the extent they left their home and business in North London and decamped to Clacton on the East coast.

So I saw out the War years without being much affected. However I do have an abiding memory from the War of the unfairness of life. At about the time I joined Collyers School a popular young master had left to join the RAF. His name was Ronald Rivaz and he became a rear gunner on a bomber, which was a job that had a life expectancy of about three weeks. Rivaz survived many sorties and became not just a hero for Collyers School but also for the nation. He wrote a successful book 'Tail Gunner' and was decorated several times and taken off active duties and given a high profile desk job recruiting for the RAF. He was only in this job for a few months when he stepped under a bus in Brighton and was killed instantly.

Chapter 3 - Teens

I went to Collyers Grammar School, Hurst Road, Horsham in September 1941 when I was ten and a half years old even though the normal age for joining Collyers was eleven plus years. I must have done spectacularly well in the entrance examination as I went straight into the second year Form Two where the average age was something like twelve and a half years old.

All my fellow pupils in this class were at least a year older than me and had spent the previous year in Form One, known as the Ants, and had a year's lessons in Latin and French, neither of which I'd even heard of. This put me at a bit of a disadvantage with the result that I came near the bottom of the class for the first two terms. This earned me the wrath of Tharp, the Headmaster who accused me of being lazy and likely to be expelled. As a punishment, for the third term of the first year I was subjected to the public humiliation of being put down into Form One. Here my peers had by that time done two terms of Latin and French so even then, and throughout my subsequent school career, I never really got to grips with Latin and French.

However, I had less trouble with the other subjects in Form One and managed to come in the top ten in those exams that term, which saved my bacon. I then progressed through Collyers

Chapter 3

School with relative ease and increasing success. After my second and more successful year in Form Two I went into the B stream in Form Three and by Form Four I had risen to the A stream where I stayed until the Sixth Form.

Collyers School was run on Public School lines, it was divided into four houses and they were controlled by Prefects with the power to cane and the Masters also entitled to inflict any punishment including beatings by cane that they wished, compulsory sports outside of normal school hours and lots of cold showers. Tharp's origins had given him some pretty high level chums, including Field Marshall Montgomery, hero of El Alamein, the Desert Rats and subsequent conduct of the War. Montgomery awarded prizes once during the latter stages of the War at the annual Founders Day prize giving ceremony at the school. This was a singular honour for our school.

In each form in the school I was among, if not the, youngest in my year form. I was also very irresponsible and in fairly constant trouble for minor misdemeanours, so that I had the unique distinction of being beaten in every year of my school career including third year Sixth when I was caught carving my initials into the school's stone main entrance door frame. These initials are still clearly visible more than fifty years later.

Of course I did not realise it at the time but in retrospect I know the life lessons I learnt at

Collyers, which were to form standards and ground rules for the rest of my life, were far more important than the academic matters.

'Pat' Tharp MA the Headmaster, a St Paul's School old boy and Christ College Oxford graduate ran Collyers as a public school with mainly dayboys. His teaching and ancillary staff were all either too old or unfit for wartime service but had been honed by service in top flight pre-war schools and were very good at their jobs. The principle on which Collyers was run was that its pupils were trained for the ruling class positions in the British Empire that had existed up until the advent of World War II. This is illustrated by the careers advisor, a teacher named Henderson, who offered only three careers to Collyers boys at the end of their school days: these were a commission in the army from Sandhurst, the Church or the Civil Service. It is regrettable that the absence of these standards in ill disciplined co-educational schools of the post war education system is only too apparent in our modern society. The way Collyers was run resulted in boys with character rising from out of the crowd and some of my contemporaries went on to great things. Unfortunately close school friendships tended to be broken by National Service after which people seemed to go their own separate ways.

Collyers was really a Classics school, Latin and Greek scholars were the most highly regarded. As mentioned earlier I had continual difficulties with

Chapter 3

Latin and never took the optional Greek. I tended to do well in science subjects. After passing school certificate (the equivalent to O Levels or today's GCSE) in the eleven subjects that were compulsory, I gained the Sixth Form doing Chemistry, Physics and Biology, the teachers for which in order were Bob Greenop, who had lost a leg in World War I, Jenny Lee a rare woman teacher who also ran the school drama club and Roland Soper much younger at about thirty who had been invalided out of the army after having been wounded in the North African desert campaign. Roland Soper wore his 'desert boots' to school, footwear which I admired and which I have worn ever since (though not the same pair).

Bob Greenop was in some respects similar to my grandfather Buba and I found it easy to relate to him. This seemed to be reciprocated because Bob Greenop was always kind to me and on several occasions spoke up for me when I got into scrapes or alternatively never said anything.

One of these scrapes went down in the annals of the school as a splendid jape. In our sixth form Chemistry class we had made what I think was called 'Nitrogen Tri-iodide'. This was a mauvish liquid which when dried out on filter paper formed brown crystals. Once dry these crystals each exploded with a sharp crack if touched. At the end of the school year there was a special all boys and masters assembly in the main hall where always the same hymns were sung to the accompaniment of the school piano played by Sutton the music master. On the penultimate day of this particular year I and my chum Griffin made a quantity of this Nitrogen Tri-iodide and after school painted this liquid onto the felt hammers of the school piano. At the assembly on the mid day following Sutton tried to play the introduction to the first hymn, only every key emitted a loud crack, a broken note and puff of violet smoke from the top of the piano. Staff were stunned and the whole school started to laugh. Only Bob Greenop had a broad grin on his face while looking directly at me. He knew what was causing the piano's peculiar behavior and who had done it, but he never let on. Sutton had another couple of unsuccessful goes at the piano, and the hymns were sung without music.

During my early years at Collyers my best friend was Brian Smith whose father farmed Great Pollards Hill farm at Southwater near Horsham. I spent a lot of time at this farm and with this experience I used to work on other farms during the school summer holiday for miniscule wages in order to have at least some money to augment my twelve and a half pence pocket money from my parents, to buy things I wanted. Father Smith used to go in his Austin 12-4 heavy car with a small trailer on the back with his wife, Brian's younger sister and Brian and I to farm sales, which seemed to occur fairly often during the War. I cannot recollect why this happened when

Chapter 3

the Government were constantly asking for an increase in home food production, but I do remember these sales as being very sad affairs.

They were normally two-day events, the animals, farm equipment, etc were sold on one day and everything, and I do mean everything, in the house the other day. It was as if the previous occupants had just walked out.

The auctioneers made lots out of the larger items of the house contents but smaller less valuable junk items were grouped together as one lot. These composite lots were sometimes in mine or Brian's price bracket. On one occasion I bought an elephant's foot umbrella stand which I thought was stuffed with sticks and things. When we tipped it out we found a folding four-ten shotgun (a poacher's gun), three fishing rods, three or four farmer's walking sticks with carved animal head handles and various other items. At another sale we bought an ancient motorcycle which, with the help of one of Father Smith's farm labourers we managed to get to run and ride round the farm as at thirteen or fourteen years old we were too young to get a licence. This bike came to an untimely end. We had seen in Boy's Own, a comic, a piece about motorcycle ice racing in Scandinavia where the rear wheel of those bikes had spikes to grip the ice. At this time there was a very sharp cold spell for some weeks so we decided to make our motorbike into an ice racer. We pushed nails through the rear tyre and then filled the tyre with concrete as nail heads had punctured the normal inner tube. With the concrete set and the back mud guard removed we rode this bike around the duck pond in the middle of the farmyard but only with our feet down, we never mastered riding it with our feet up. The end of this was when a thaw set in and the ice was made even more slippery by a layer of water on the surface, I was riding round on the pond when the bike slipped sideways into the corner of a stone built cowshed which projected into the pond. I hurt myself and had to be carried indoors to be patched up by Mrs Smith. The bike lay where it fell. The next morning the ice had melted completely and the bike had disappeared. We were never able to get the bike out, it's probably still in that pond today.

I used to bicycle with Brian the three or so miles to the farm in order to play after school. The route was along Kerves Lane in Horsham and up Bourne Hill, an incline too steep for boys to ride up on a bicycle. The road at Bourne Hill had on one side a steep bank with a dense and high hedge at the top and on the other side was a wood stretching back some distance. In this wood near the top of the hill there was a sweet chestnut tree.

At the appropriate time of the year Brian and I would have a breather from pushing our bikes up the hill and go into the wood and collect sweet chestnuts on the ground still in their prickly husks. The technique for getting nuts out of the husks was to roll the husks under your foot.

Chapter 3

There was so much soft leaf mould in the wood that rolling did not work so we used to carry armfuls of husks out into the road, roll them on the hard surface and then pocket the nuts to take home for cooking on a bonfire.

My parents would not let me have lights on my bike as they thought this would encourage me to get home at a reasonable time. Of course, I always left Brian's farm too late and rode home in the dark. On this particular occasion I came round the corner at the top of Bourne Hill flat out in the dark so that I could freewheel the mile or so down the hill to the river, and I ran full pelt into something in the road. I went over the handlebars and I can recall my face hitting coarse fur very hard. As I landed in the road I looked up and saw, silhouetted against the night sky, a full size stag, antlers and all, taking off from a standing start and clearing the bank and hedge in one leap. The top of the hedge must have been twelve feet above road level. This stag had been eating the chestnut husks we had left in the road on the way out earlier. The stag mangled the front wheel of my bike so, although I had sprained my left wrist and had scrapes and bruises, I had to half carry my bike the mile and a half home.

While at Brian Smith's farm I thought I had found a business opportunity. In those days wheat was harvested in stukes, which are bundles of wheat gathered into armfuls bound with twisted straw and stood up in groups in the fields. These were picked up and taken to the farmyard and laid on a bed of hedge cuttings to form a corn stack, which had a tarpaulin cover on top, awaiting the threshing contractor with his steam traction engine and threshing equipment who travelled from farm to farm. There were no combine harvesters in those days.

The stack being threshed was a big day on the farm and the family gathered to watch the proceedings. On this particular year the stack was almost done when Brian and I noticed a lot of mice in the bottom layer, now this was not unusual except that in this case the mice were a bright ginger colour not the normal grey/brown. Sensing a business opportunity we gathered up as many of these mice as we could and put them in a big cardboard box. We then looked for somewhere to put the box which gave an additional layer of security. We hit on the family car, the Austin 12-4 heavy, and so put the box on the back seat.

Being canny enough not to flood the market we took about six mice to school each day and sold them at six pence each as pet mice as the colour was not that of wild mice. They sold like hot cakes but when we went to collect the fourth batch we found the big cardboard box had a hole and was empty. That was the end of the business venture except whenever the family went out in the car after that they said that the back seat needed oiling as continuous squeaking was heard from it.

Chapter 3

They never knew it was ginger mice living in the upholstery.

I still have a permanent reminder of Brian Smith in the form of a twisted finger on my left hand. This came about when I was sitting on an old collapsed five bar gate with a finger in one of the empty peg holes when Brian attacked me from behind pulling me off the gate with my finger still in the hole. My finger broke between the top and middle knuckles. We had both been in trouble after some misdemeanour and decided it would be better not to tell parents about the finger. In those days small boys could not go to doctors or hospitals without parents and possibly police being involved. So we splinted the finger with wood strips and bandaged it up and after a few painful weeks it healed up but after the swelling had gone down it was apparent that it had been set slightly twisted out of line. It remains like that to this day.

Brian Smith was not very academic and while he and I were together when I was in the B stream when I rose to the A stream our ways parted, although we remained good friends. My new chums were a more intelligent dilettante set which originated in the teacher Jenny Lee's drama club. This I joined not because I had any aspirations to act but because members of this club were able to go and camp for a week in Stratford on Avon each year to go to the theatre to see Shakespeare plays. This outing was not accompanied by any teacher.

We were transported in a removal van owned and driven by the father of one of our leading members, John Hempstead, but left unsupervised for a week.

I celebrated this great freedom by wearing a Black Watch regimental kilt, bought at an army surplus store, and a monocle for a bit of extra class. I spent most of the week becoming proficient at punting on the river and drinking rough cider in a pub displaying outside a sign with the Black Swan on one side and a Dirty Duck on the other. It was at this stage of my life I began to get very interested in girls.

My particular chum in this group with whom I shared ownership of a Calthorpe motorcycle, was Eric Thompson, star of several school productions, who wanted to become a professional actor. Poor Eric, who was a most inoffensive fellow, suffered from a face like that of an old punch drunk boxer. Apparently he'd looked like that from birth – and he'd never been in a fight in his life. Leading male actors both screen and stage in those days were conventionally handsome with little moustaches and Brylcreemed hair. After National Service Eric went to drama school and while unable to get much acting work he saw, and then managed to buy, the rights to a French children's cartoon programme. Eric renamed the programme 'Magic Roundabout' and spoke all the characters in English. It was a huge success on

Chapter 3

BBC television and ran for many years until Eric died – of which more elsewhere.

I lost touch with Eric when he moved to London and subsequently married and started a family. Then, some years later in the early sixties, British Rail went on one of their periodic strikes which prevented me getting to and from work. The solution was to stay with school chum Peter Broderick and his three older sisters, all of whom had left Horsham when their father, manager of Dolcis shoe shop, had died and were then living in a big house in Highgate. This I did for a few weeks. One evening I went out for a walk on Hampstead Heath and bumped into Eric Thompson. Eric invited me to dinner a couple of days later and I went and met his wife and daughter, then about four years old, whose name was Emma and her baby sister. Emma Thompson is now a famous Oscar winning Hollywood actress famed in Britain, America and particularly Hollywood.

Peter Broderick was a friend and school contemporary of mine and, while of a retiring nature and not one of the dilettante set, was much involved in back stage activities with the School drama group. Before I lost touch with him in the later sixties Peter had found a successful career in the film world by making and directing information films for the Government.

Another dramatic connection from this period was that I was in the Collyers school tennis team.

We used to play odd matches with other boys schools but the highlight of our year was when we were invited annually to play the girls at Herons Ghyll, a very exclusive private girls school in St Leonards Road, Horsham who could not find any exclusive girls to play locally and had to resort to common boys from the grammar school. These girls all seemed very attractive, probably it was the smell of money.

One in particular I got to know slightly was named Virginia McKenna. This girl became a film star in a very very successful film called 'Born Free', married her co-star Bill Travers and lived at Coldharbour in the lee of Leith Hill, Dorking. Born Free was about a lioness named Elsa and making the film in Africa had such an impact on both stars that they started the Born Free Foundation, a charity that helps wild animals worldwide. This organisation was very successful and grew over the years, since Bill Travers died it has been run by Virginia and their son Will. In the 1980s when one of my offices, 3 Grove House, became available it was leased by Born Free. The negotiations were carried out by Will Travers who was much taken aback when, at the completion of the deal, I asked to be remembered to his mother as a tennis opponent from her school days. Much to my surprise he later confirmed that she did remember me and particularly my forehand smash! But I think she was just being kind to an old man.

Chapter 3

Born Free are still my tenants and are now in both numbers 2 and 3 Grove House.

The Drama Club friends fancied themselves as genteel 'coffee' set and so after school each day we would meet up in the café on the first floor of the Odeon Cinema to drink coffee and smoke either Balkan Sobranie or Turkish Pink Pasha cigarettes. On Saturday mornings we transferred to Wakefield Café in West Street, Horsham, a fashionable meeting place where there were girls to chat up. Occasionally we would go to the Olde Punche Bowle Café in Middle Street, Horsham, because it was run by very pretty twin sisters only slightly older than us. None of my group ever got anywhere with these two girls, however it was while in this café that there was an unusual occurrence.

This café building was medieval and the first floor projected out about one metre in front of the ground floor. On the opposite side of the very narrow Middle Street was Tanner & Chart a big drapers shop, which had a similar projecting first floor. On the build up to D-Day, when the allies crossed the channel to France, the land and woods around Horsham accommodated lots of troops and equipment. Their weapon collection included Canadians with Sherman tanks and these tanks used to drive around like cars do today, going to the pub and going to see some girls. We were in the Olde Punche Bowle Café on the first floor one day when there was a terrible graunching sound and a lot of shouting and the little windows were obscured by something outside. We looked out as best we could and found that one of those Canadian tanks had tried to drive up Middle Street and the turret had jammed between the two projecting first floors. We were able to evacuate the building by squeezing past the tank tracks and then we could get an end view of the situation. The shape of the upper part of the tank was a perfect fit between the projecting first floors of the two buildings and there it was stuck fast. I believe the army engineers dragged the tank out backwards the following day. The damage to the Olde Punche Bowle was only superficial but that to Tanner & Chart was more serious and required some rebuilding works.

These tanks for D-Day were accompanied by tank recovery transporters which were massive multi wheeled articulated vehicles of enormous weight empty, so with a tank onboard they were prodigiously heavy and broke up the road surface and shook buildings as they passed. This feature got me a new bicycle. I could never afford a decent bike and rode around on various old bicycles. On this particular occasion I had walked, talking to a High School girl, to Horsham station outside which there was a roundabout. I had nonchalantly stood the bike at the kerb when along came one of these loaded tank transporters, and as it came round the roundabout the vibration caused my bike to slip down and out

Chapter 3

into the road where it was run over by the outer row of wheels of the transporter. The lower half of the bike was crushed, I do not mean bent, I mean crushed. The bike was irreparable. Notification to the army ultimately produced for me a brand new Hercules bike which was a great improvement on the old one.

Our small coffee set was well known amongst the young people of Horsham, particularly the girls. The belle of Horsham was Betty Spratt a stunning blonde who worked in Trevor Cales the chemists on the Carfax and she joined our set on various Saturday night and Sunday adventures. I always thought she was outside my league so never made any advances to her. She became and remains, sixty plus years later, a good friend whom I see fairly regularly. After an engagement of fourteen years Betty Spratt married Keith Gray and went to live in Nuthurst.

Our social set met up during term time. During the school holidays, particularly the six-week summer one, except for our very close chums we all went our separate ways. In my case this meant going to Lodge Hill, the West Sussex County Council Residential Centre at Watersfield, south of Pullborough, where week long courses in various wholesome subjects were run on a continuous basis during the school summer holidays. These courses ranged from the ecology of the Amberley Wild Brooks, through watercolour painting and trug making onto athletics and drama. None of these courses interested me but what got me to go to the Lodge Hill every week during the school summer holidays was that half of the sixty or so attendees were girls.

The way the courses operated was that we had lectures and demonstrations on the subject during each morning and after lunch we were free to do what we liked and there were evening events, mainly social, and a dance on the last night of the week. The serious students in the subjects were virtually non-existent. The boys and girls were from all over West Sussex and came for exactly the same reason as me. To meet each other. I used to sign up for every course which meant staying at Lodge Hill for some six weeks every summer. I used to send dirty laundry home on the bus each Saturday and receive clean clothes back the same way again each week. At Lodge Hill there was an inexhaustible supply of girlfriends and I made many semi-permanent relationships, which continued long after the courses finished. I had one or more girlfriends in every significant town in Sussex and most of the villages.

One of these I remember very well was Margaret Capsey who lived on a farm near Cowfold, south of Horsham. Now Margaret Capsey was a talented athlete who competed at Youth National level. She could run faster than me and our tennis games were long and close fought battles. In trying to keep up with Margaret Capsey

Chapter 3

I developed a propensity for cramp in my legs. She knew of this problem and if present would vigorously rub the affected part which helped.

On the occasion that comes to mind we had played hard tennis almost all of a summer's afternoon and went for tea and cakes in the Odeon café and decided to go to the Capitol cinema, the local fleapit picture house built to imitate a South American hacienda which was cheaper than the main cinemas, the Odeon and the Ritz and showed art and foreign films. We had not long settled into the cinema when I got severe cramp and contraction of the thigh muscles of my left leg which promptly shot out straight in front of me, my foot punched through the thin plywood back of the seat in front of me and pushed the chap seated in it to the floor which allowed the seat base to tip up locking my leg in position. The seat back breaking made a noise and the chap's shouts as he was knocked to the floor brought the usherette with a torch and ultimately the manager out at a run. Meanwhile Margaret had dropped onto her knees beside me and was rubbing my upper left leg furiously.

The film was stopped and the house lights put on but I still had a hell of a job getting my leg out of the broken seat back, even after the seat base had been held down, due to the sharp splintered ply acting like barbs. The manager ejected us from the cinema and banned us from ever going there again.

This leg cramp business was a bit of nuisance. I had joined the Horsham Cycling Club who ran time trials of five and ten miles down the A24 Worthing Road starting from the top of Tower Hill at, I recall, six o clock on a Sunday morning. I kitted myself out in skinny black vest and shorts and stripped everything not essential from my bike and went off to race. Unfortunately every Saturday night I was out dancing or jollying and I did not get home until the early hours. I would fall into bed to be woken by my alarm, seemingly only minutes later, to go off and race on my bicycle. I left home without any breakfast and not even a cup of tea and had to ride hard to even make the start on time.

I would complete the trial and come home to join the family having breakfast, during which I would be attacked by cramp in each calf muscle and each thigh muscle in turn. A lump like a golf ball would rise in the muscle, it was excruciating as it was coming up and a bad ache while it was up and it hurt like hell going down about five minutes later. This process was so painful that the sweat poured off me and I ground my teeth. Somebody told me that I could prevent cramp if I ate sugar. I bought some thick syrupy concoction from a chemist, which I drank through a rubber tube from a metal bottle on the handlebar of my bike, this did nothing except make me feel sick. So I reluctantly gave up cycle racing. But unfortunately I found out later that the biking

Chapter 3

cramps had had a permanent effect making me prone to leg and toe cramps which I have suffered from periodically all my life.

The Margaret Capsey incident in the Capitol was not the first time I'd been in trouble in that cinema. About a year before the leg-through-seat incident, my friends Johnny Thomas and Johnny Hull and I thought we should try and present a more mature image by smoking pipes. We each managed to acquire a pipe but could not afford proper pipe tobacco. Johnny Hull found an advertisement in Exchange & Mart for mail order herbal tobacco at a price we could afford so we sent away for some. It arrived in a large brown paper bag and looked like dried hedge leaves. We could not smoke our pipes in public or at home so we went to the Capitol cinema on a Saturday evening when a popular film had filled the cinema. We were lucky to get three seats together in the middle of the auditorium where once settled we each filled our pipes with this herbal tobacco and lit up. The pipe contents caught fire, a bit like a miniature bonfire and spat glowing embers in all directions whilst crackling. These flying embers cleared the three rows in front and ten feet either side of us before we managed to knock the pipes out on the floor and pocket them. Unfortunately the heap of herbal tobacco continued to burn on the floor like a small bonfire. Again the manager turned up and accused us of lighting a fire in his cinema, and when we could see by his torchlight the size of the smoke cloud we had created I could understand his attitude. We were thrown out and gave up pipe smoking there and then.

I obtained a Higher School Certificate in three science subjects, adequate for a university place, and got my name on the coveted Role of Honour Plaque which still hangs in the School Hall – now the Library.

For several years in my mid-teens I had to wear a wire brace on a plate to pull my projecting top front teeth back into a more suitable place. This was done by a dentist on Horsham Carfax named Ellis Kent to whom I had to go, I think, weekly for nearly two years to have this wire brace tightened. A very uncomfortable process. Ellis Kent was a big fat jolly man with a false metal leg to replace the one he lost in World War One.

Ellis Kent had a son Michael, who was a couple of years younger than me and who I knew quite well as he married an ex girlfriend of mine, Gabi Rojek. Michael became a dental Mechanic (Technician) with his own firm, making false teeth in a semi-derelict shed in the centre of Chichester.

In the late 1960s when I had my own Consulting Engineering practice and West Sussex County Council were our biggest client, I happened to mention to Michael Kent at some social function that I was having trouble with my denture carrying my upper front teeth, the original teeth having been knocked out some years before. In those days professional

Chapter 3

restrictions prevented you from going directly to a dental mechanic, you had to go through a dentist. However, Michael Kent said if I called in at his workshop in Chichester he would make me his best quality "lightweight racing" metal denture for free.

In the late morning on a beautiful summer's day after a meeting at the County Hall in Chichester, I called on Michael Kent who took an impression of my upper jaw using a large semi-circular metal mould and setting mould material. A quite normal procedure. However, taking impressions was not normal for Michael Kent. He left the mould in for far too long, and neither he nor I could remove it. Michael telephoned a local dentist chum who agreed to remove this moulding. Unfortunately, this dentist was at the opposite end of the pedestrianised centre of Chichester, and immediately opposite County Hall.

So with Michael Kent leading the way, and me looking like a Frankenstein monster with the mould sticking out of my mouth, we set off walking through the centre of Chichester just as County Hall employees were coming out for their lunch hour. I had to run the gauntlet of my clients nodding and grunting. The dentist managed to remove the mould without pulling out any of my natural teeth with it, and Michael Kent made me a super denture which I used for more than forty years.

However, my standing in County Hall was never the same as before.

Michael Kent lived with his wife Gabi in Southwater, and was an enthusiast for fast cars in which he commuted to Chichester. A few years after the dental impression fiasco, Michael Kent was sadly killed when he crashed his Ford Capri 3 Litre on his way to work.

At this stage, ending my secondary school period, I had to make up my mind as to what career I wanted in adult life. I did not fancy any of the careers offered by the Collyers Careers Master which were the Army, the Church or the Civil Service. Visiting a dentist regularly I became conscious that here was somebody earning their living doing something practical. I decided that probably being a dentist would suit me.

My father could not afford to send me to University dental school for some four years so I applied to West Sussex County Council for a grant. Part of this application was a report from your Headmaster as to his opinion on your suitability. Simultaneously, I applied to the London Dental Hospital and Guy's Hospital Dental School. I was accepted at both. However, I was notified by West Sussex County Council that the report from Tharp said I was too young and irresponsible to benefit from college before National Service, but I would be awarded a grant after National Service when I would be older and more sensible. Even at the time I knew Tharp was

Chapter 3

right and so I accepted National Service quite willingly. The National Service entrance procedure was that you were called for a medical and aptitude tests before being allocated to one of the armed services.

I was called to Brighton for my medical tests.

On the entry form I was asked for my preferred army regiment. I entered the Tank Corps because I fancied driving a tank and the Household Cavalry because of the uniform and riding round on horses in London impressing the girls.

In addition to the actual medical there was a practical test consisting of assembling an electrical three pin plug on a length of flexible cable and, with other people, a half hour written test with a book, on each page of which were groups of patterns with one in the series missing and about six separate choices from which you had to chose the missing shape. The man in charge kept repeating and emphasising that you wrote your name in the top left hand corner and the date, etc. After going over this several times he said, "Before you start is there anyone here who cannot read or write?" Imagine my astonishment when out of the twenty or so people there, two said they could neither read nor write. I could not believe it. When the test started I sailed through it and finished in about fifteen minutes. I was an arrogant little tick.

However, I was very impressed when I was subsequently posted to the Royal Electrical and

Mechanical Engineers (REME), a regiment I had never even heard of. To this day I do not know how the very crude and simple tests had revealed to the examiner that I was a potential engineer. However, I am eternally grateful to the Army for determining this bent which has been the focus of my life ever since.

CHAPTER 4

National Service and Hadens

In the period between the end of school in July and November, when I went into the army, I got a job as a postman (a continuation of work offered to senior Collyers boys which I had done for the previous two or three Chistmases). This entailed starting at 6.00am and finishing at lunchtime for six days a week. I enjoyed the work and managed to write off two Post Office bicycles by riding recklessly. The main advantage of this job was the free afternoons for which I enrolled at Horsham Art School in Hurst Road run by a chap called Wimble who I had come across at Lodge Hill and with whom I got on very well.

With my latent and then unrecognized penchant for work with my hands, I took up sculpting. The only student, I was given space in the Basement, tools and materials and set to work. I did several pieces with which Wimble and I were pleased. Wimble entered one piece in an exhibition where it won a prize after I had gone into the Army. A couple of these pieces are still around at home.

While at Art School I was asked if I would sit for the Life Class. I agreed, provided I kept my clothes on. One of the students was a chap called Streeter who did an oil portrait of me which he subsequently presented to me. I framed that picture and still have it, an artist's impression of me when I was eighteen years old.

My army service started in November 1949 with me being sent for basic training to REME Blandford camp in Dorset. Each monthly intake was about one hundred and fifty national servicemen recruits, all accommodated in a complex of huts known as spiders, some thirty to each dormitory.

The dormitory allocation was purely alphabetical so although REME is a technical corps my mix of room mates ranged from graduate engineers to a pig breeder from Hartlepool who could only read and sign cheques (at which he must have been very good as he had a lot more money than anybody else). However, in the six weeks of basic training with these people I learnt a lot about human nature and most importantly that if you accepted the Army's little ways life was bearable, if you rebelled and got awkward things got very difficult and unpleasant.

Towards the end of basic training, certain of us, including me, were separated off to do an examination to see if we were commissioned officer material. I apparently passed this test and at the end of basic training I was sent to Honiton in Devon to do a four week pre-officer cadet training unit (OCTU) course. This course was a

Chapter 4

very different proposition to my earlier basic training. It was obvious that the army did not have a great need for National Service officers and this pre OCTU course was run by officers who had a very tough time rising from the ranks during the War and thought that everyone aspiring to be an officer should suffer to an equivalent degree.

In consequence, this course was arranged to break even the toughest. At each 6am morning parade we were offered ND forms, that is signing out as being Non Desirous of being an officer, which would immediately release us from the course. In addition things were arranged so that we only got three hours' sleep each night after hard physical activity all day. It was December, bitterly cold, the huts were heated by one slow combustion stove which we could not light because the stove had to be black boot polished bright, and the coal in the bucket whitewashed without any black showing at 5.30am every morning.

The ablutions only had cold water. I cut my face with a rusty razor blade one morning, this became infected and I ended up with impetigo which created a huge scab all round my mouth which cracked painfully if I spoke or ate. I had to report sick and had some violet substance smeared over my face twice a day. As reporting sick was automatic disqualification from the course I dropped out after three weeks. Of the thirty people from various regiments that started the course with me only one passed out at the end and he was a thirty year old regular soldier, a paratrooper, who had been through the War. He was very tough.

From Honiton I was sent to AAC-AAC Command School of Technical Instruction based in Lydd in Kent for a nine month course to be a Craftsman Technician. This was an entirely different proposition from Honiton. All the students were nice well educated lads and the whole camp was run on relaxed lines appropriate to a technical college, which it really was. Of course, there were fundamental army rules to be complied with but if you toed the line you had a good life.

I spent nine months at Lydd with classroom lessons and workshop practical on electrical elements of anti-aircraft equipment, searchlights and guns. I took to that like a duck to water. I had a thoroughly good time and did well without any real effort.

The School had a voluntary athletics team which I thought it would be fun to join, not least because team members got various privileges, and sometimes special food. There were already team members for the ordinary events like sprinting, long distance running and jumping who were much better than I but there were vacancies in the less usual field events that, in those days were normally not covered by state schools. As there was nobody to compare me with I was accepted

Chapter 4

into the team as discus thrower. We used to train one afternoon a week and during my time with the team we went three times to compete in the Southern Command Athletics competitions with other Army units always held on a Friday.

One of those trips stands out in my memory. The event was staged at the United Services Sports Ground at Chatham which was a proper facility with a NAAFI hostel where one could spend the night. We had a couple of hours journey in the back of a Bedford three ton army truck, not only very uncomfortable but full of exhaust fumes which did not improve the athletes' performance. We arrived at the hostel where there were toilets which we all needed. I went in with the others beside our shot putter, a big lad from York. When we had done what we had to, using usual stall urinals, our shot putter saw a row of automatic flush wall mounted bowl urinals.

"What are these things?" he said.

"Oh," said somebody, "they are for washing your feet".

"Great" says the shot putter taking off one shoe and sock and putting his foot in the bowl "where are the taps?" he asked.

"It's all automatic," he was told.

We left him there with his foot in the urinal; he did not appear for some time.

When the event was over we were given the choice of going straight on weekend leave or going back to camp in the lorry. Living in the South

East I opted to go home. With another team member we got onto the A2 road to London and we got a lift in a lorry carrying, I recall, five huge rolls of paper, like giant toilet rolls each weighing 3 or 4 tons, destined for the newspaper printing presses in London's Fleet Street. Each roll of paper was about five feet in diameter and some eight feet wide, the five held on the lorry by chains.

The road dropped down and rose steeply for regular towns located on little estuaries on the banks of the Thames. Climbing up from one of these dips in the road there was a bang as both chains holding the paper rolls failed and three rolls fell off the back of the lorry. The end of one roll caught a lamppost and stopped, slewed round, against the front of a shop, the other two went off back down the hill, one demolished a car, the other to came harmlessly to rest the other side of the town centre.

The poor driver was terribly upset but after I and my chum had spoken to the Police we were released and continued homeward.

An interesting interlude during my time at Lydd was when a film company virtually took over the Camp for several weeks to make a film using the army personnel as extras. The film was called The Dark Man and featured up and coming actors and actresses. I think, the male lead was named Maxwell Reed, but he was an alcoholic so never came to anything after this one film. There were

Chapter 4

two girl starlets, one was named Natasha Parry the other's name I cannot recall.

To be involved, albeit marginally, and seeing a film made was fascinating. The story, as I remember it, was very simple, the male lead was seen committing a murder by the two girls who were actresses in a local repertory company. They told the police who set about hunting down the killer while the killer set about tracking down the two girl witnesses in order to dispose of them.

Most of the film was shot outdoors in or around Lydd Camp and out on the pebble flat marshes.

In some parts most of the camp were out being filmed for mass searches of the marshes. I, like most others, was in this crowd.

Later there were a number of scenes with only a few soldiers and the easy people to get for these parts were members of the athletics team as they were somewhat outside the daily camp routine. I figured in this select group not because of my good looks or acting ability, both non-existent, but because I had under my charge a Mk 8 trailer mounted carbon-arc search light which was written into the script for the final dramatic scenes. So I, with several others, was with the film crew after the rest of the camp had returned to normal duties.

I certainly saw how complicated making a film was. I could not understand why they compounded these complications by filming scenes out of chronological order. The person in the film crew who impressed me most was the Continuity Girl who could remember the position of the sun, the cloud formation etc for the next take of a scene shot days before. She did this with just notes on a clip-board, no stills camera or other visual record.

At about 10.30 each evening, after any normal film showing in the Lydd Town tiny shed-like cinema was over, the film people took over and showed themselves the day's filming which they called Rushes to see if it was acceptable or would have to be done again. We lads from the camp could go down and see these Rushes. Initially a lot did but the novelty soon wore off and certainly I stopped going.

Eventually filming was completed but before final clearing up and departure the film people, purely by chance, asked me and two of my athletics team chums if we would each get a rifle and pose for some still camera shots. We duly turned out fully dressed with rifles. A stills camera man was lying on his back in a shallow trench dug in the pebbles and we were asked to run in line abreast and jump over him. This he would photograph. We did this three or four times. The film people then packed up and went away.

My life returned to normal and the film thing went to the back of my mind.

Imagine my astonishment when, some months later, going home across London by Underground

Chapter 4

Train, in the foot tunnel at Victoria Station there was a poster advertising The Dark Man on the wall featuring me and my two chums with rifles leaping in the air.

Our figures were not far off life size and I was instantly recognizable, not just to me, but I was told so by lots of people who saw this poster which was plastered all over London and later filtered down to Horsham. My mother was telephoned a good deal by fans. I was back in Lydd.

Lydd is on Romney Marshes which was then and probably still is a most extraordinary place. Lydd is about three miles from the sea at Dungeness. Romney Marsh all round the Lydd area and down to the sea is not a marsh in the general sense at all but is a pebble flat unbroken by anything but occasional ditches called dykes.

To the west, the nearest habitation was about three miles away, a shanty village called Camber Sands, which had been evacuated during the war as it was indefensible from sea-borne landings. When I was at Lydd there was only two inhabitants at Camber, a squatting artist and his statuesque daughter who a lot of chaps tried to get to know without any success. One reason for this girl's popularity was that she used to swim without clothes from the huge beach at Camber.

Unfortunately we were always in camp at army activity when she swam.

I had a very nice girlfriend named Daisy who was the daughter of the one and only postman in Lydd village. She had lived in Lydd all her life and showed me aspects of Romney Marsh I would never have seen otherwise. I built a bicycle out of bits of old broken bikes around the camp and with this girl I used to cycle all over the area.

To get home to Horsham on leave from Lydd the normal way was a fearful journey. One had to catch the train that only ran once every three hours from Lydd on a long stopping journey to Ashford on the mainline. From Ashford you went to London, Charing Cross, then across London by tube with three changes to Victoria and down to Horsham in all three or four hours travelling. Not practical for the usual thirty six hour pass, that is Saturday lunchtime until midnight Sunday. However from Rye, which is to the west of Lydd on the edge of Romney Marsh, there was a slow but direct train to Brighton, and from there a direct train to Horsham in all only about two hours from Rye to home. From Lydd to Rye is only some seven miles by road via Camber as the crow flies, while by road it is more like ten miles, the extra miles result from the road coming out of Rye forming an enormous loop, almost a full circle, presumably to circumvent some marsh hazard.

However, there was a footpath perhaps half a mile long with single plank no handrail bridges across four or five dykes, which cut off the loop road and reduced the distance to Rye to the direct

Chapter 4

route of about seven miles. So this was the way I went home on leave. I used to ride my bike to Rye, leave it in the station yard and pick it up and ride back to camp at about 9 o'clock on Sunday night when the train from Brighton arrived.

Of course, it was dark on the Sunday night and there were no lights of any kind once you left Rye town and were on the marsh. I had not been able to find any bike lights around the camp so I rode in the dark without lights. This did not matter as there was no traffic of any kind out on the marsh, particularly on the Rye to Lydd route.

While the marsh was a flat area of pebbles, at the back of the beach the pebbles were heaped up to form a continuous bank about three feet high. This banking was probably caused by the pebbles pushed up and left by high spring tides and strong winds, and it was rather optimistically called a sea wall by the locals.

Particularly in the autumn, Romney Marsh in the Lydd area is very prone to dense low fog about three feet deep forming at night with a clean cut off at the top. Above the fog the air is crystal clear.

These fogs are a bit eerie as the sheep on the marsh lie down as they cannot see anything but the fog makes them cough with the sound exactly like that of a man coughing. On one occasion I was cycling back from Rye at night in one of these waist high fogs (but walking my bike across the plank bridges) when about fifty yards away to my left I saw a globe of light about the size of a football rising slowly up through the mist. When it reached the top of the mist it shot off at an angle to me at an incredible speed to disappear as a dot in the distance. This whole process was without a sound. This frightened the life out of me, being only one of two occasions I recall my hair standing on end.

I got on my bike and rode hell for leather to Lydd. I was so shaken I could not face going straight into camp so I went round to Daisy's house, where the family were listening to the radio. I recounted my experience and her father laughed and said I had seen a Will-o'-the-Wisp. Apparently quite common. He explained that leaves fall down and rot among the pebbles to create methane which periodically spontaneously combusts to form a ball of flame. This being hot and lighter than air, rises up to the top of the mist where there is an almost undetectable breeze of air coming from the sea over the pebble bank sea wall. The burning gas meets this breeze and burns out going downwind. The incredible speed is an optical illusion as the volume of the ball of flame rapidly reduces and appears as the perspective of supersonic speed.

Daisy and I went out on our bikes several times after this to see if we could see them. We only once saw one vaguely and a long way off.

I spent nine months at Lydd and graduated as a technician in radar and predictors (army grade Craftsman) and was posted in November to HaHa

Chapter 4

barracks in Woolwich. This was a misnomer, there was nothing funny about Woolwich. I arrived in the depths of the coldest winter in decades. HaHa barracks was an old two storey cavalry barracks where the horses were kept on the ground floor and the men lived on the first floor. The warmth of the horses allegedly kept the men warm. There were no horses when I was there and hence no heat whatsoever.

I spent my days alone in an unheated mobile workshop on the banks of the River Thames in Woolwich dockyard. The Thames at this time was polluted beyond belief. Dead animals and other rubbish would go down with the tide past my workshop in the morning and come back up again in the evening.

Not surprisingly just before Christmas I fell ill with what was diagnosed as pneumonia and I was sent off to an army sanatorium hospital set up primarily for TB cases. I was put in a ward the ceiling of which was twenty feet high and which had very tall opening windows down both sides, which were open all day long for the outdated treatment of TB. Needless to say I was not very comfortable in this hospital and being anxious to get home for Christmas I claimed to be better than I was and was released on leave on Christmas Eve. After largely recovering at home, when I returned after the short Christmas break I applied for a posting away from Woolwich. This was granted and I went to the Radar Research &

Development Establishment (RRDE) at Malvern, Worcestershire. This was a civilian establishment where some one thousand young men, mainly graduates worked. They lived in a purpose built hostel called Geraldine, which consisted of ranges of huts not dissimilar to an army camp. Within RRDE was a small REME unit consisting of nine people of which I was one.

Our commanding officer was a Major Logan who we saw very little of as he was a keen sailor with a very nice fifty foot sailing yacht, wartime booty from the Germans, on which he spent most of his time. There were two young second lieutenants, one of which was Thomason – of whom more later – two retirement age staff sergeants and then two craftsmen and two other general dogsbody privates.

The lower ranks were given a choice of living in the Geraldine hostel or being paid a little more and finding digs in Malvern. All the digs allowance would run to was a very tatty place which, although my chum Geoff Singer preferred it, I did not fancy so I opted for the hostel, a very good choice as it turned out.

Looking back I am astonished at the responsibility I and my fellow craftsman Geoff Singer were given. We each had a mobile workshop and the occasional use of a driver and some four different models of radar sets under our charge. We installed modifications notified by the radar manufacturers or recreated defects or faults

Chapter 4

advised from the field and wrote up the alterations and corrective measures to be inserted in the respective manuals called 'electrical and mechanical engineering regulations' (EMERS), for issue to all the REME workshops. We were left alone with virtually no supervision, other than being chased to keep to deadlines.

Our little group had access to a small civilian workshop with a range of machine tools run by a couple of chaps a little older than us. Here I was helped to make simple bits for Thomason's car, of which more later. It was with this workshop I made a discovery which should have made me a millionaire if I had not been in the Army. In the early radar sets of those days the signal was transported from the set to the aerial in a rectangular copper pipe called a wave guide. To avoid distortion of the wave form and hence incorrect radar imaging, the internal shape and form of the bends of this wave guide were critical to a very high degree. The making of these wave guides was a patented process held by the manufacturers who charged the Army exorbitant fees and a very long delivery for replacement wave guides required due to any mechanical damage or necessary modifications to the set.

One day, having a cup of tea with the lads in the workshop they played a joke on me. My teaspoon disappeared in my tea. The lads in the workshop showed me some material called Woods metal that they had scrounged to make joke teaspoons. Woods metal at room temperatures looked and handled a little like pewter but in hot water it melts. The workshop boys had made a mould in the shape of teaspoon and by pouring Woods metal into the mould they were able to create what felt and looked like a normal teaspoon. However stir your hot tea with this spoon and all you were left with was the bit you were holding. A one time joke. I was intrigued and spent time playing around with this solid Woods metal. I found it could be machined to a very fine tolerance. I persuaded my boss, Captain Thomason to get a quantity of Woods metal which I and the workshop lads cast up and machined to a wave guide form and then heavily electro copper plated. After plating the piece was put in hot water and the Woods metal drained out to leave a perfect internal wave guide shape. This technique was adopted by the Army and our little unit, but not me, got the credit. Subsequently radar sets with wave guides were superseded by more modern sets where wave guides are not needed.

When I was called up the duration of National Service was eighteen months. As mentioned earlier I had a money grant and a place at two Dental Schools fixed for the autumn after I finished National Service. However, while I was in the army the Government extended the duration to two years (I think this was because at that time we were fighting in Malaya). This extension took my Service beyond the University start dates. In

Chapter 4

this circumstance you applied for an early release to go to college. You can imagine the fuss and form filling this entailed. Anyway my early release application was accepted and I was given a demobilisation date in early September.

I had about a week's leave due so I came home and only had to return for a couple of days for my release. I made contact with West Sussex County Council to claim my grant promised after National Service, only to be told that central Government policy had changed while I was in the army and grants were no longer available after National Service. Needless to say I was much put out about this and decided to take the matter higher. In my Army uniform I caught the 'workman's' train at 06.15am from Horsham to London where I arrived about 8 o'clock. I walked to Whitehall and the Ministry of Education only to find that it did not open until 9 o'clock. I sat on the entrance steps and went in with the arriving staff. At the reception I said I wanted to see the Minister of Education who was a Labour MP by the name of Florence Horsborough.

Of course, I was told that was not possible and I was fobbed off with some junior clerk. However after making a lot of fuss throughout the day I passed through many hands until at about 4 o'clock in the afternoon I did get to see Ms Horsborough. She sat in an office about a hundred yards long with huge arched windows and a carpet you had to wade through. She sympathised with my plight and said she would try and make an exception for me and provide the grant.

I went home and thought about the betrayal by West Sussex County Council and decided that, after discovering engineering in the army, I really did not want to become a dentist so I returned to the army at the end of my leave and told them I no longer wanted early release. You can imagine the ructions this caused. However I did stay in the army for a total of two years until November 1951.

After my National Service, to earn money while I planned how to become an engineer, I took a job at the British Coal Utilisation Association (BCURA) at Leatherhead as a laboratory assistant analysing various coal samples.

My father mentioned where I was working to a railway friend of his who was the Chief Heating and Ventilating Engineer for the Southern region of British Rail who used the services of BCURA to select fuels for coal fired plants then still in common use. This chap was named Fred (Peter) Foreman and on a visit to BCURA one very hot summer day called into my laboratory in a single storey hut to have a word. I was very hot and sweaty and very busy and not realising who he was I told him he would have to wait until I had completed the analysis I was working on. This must have impressed him because when we chatted later he said he might be able to get me in on a training scheme with G N Haden & Sons Ltd,

Chapter 4

the biggest heating and ventilating contractors in the country.

He was as good as his word and I joined Hadens as 'Post Graduate' on a three year training scheme, which included one year full time at college – now London South Bank University. In fact there were only ever two other of these post graduate trainees at Hadens, all other staff coming from apprenticeships.

Anyway I realised my luck and worked hard and passed the college diploma (now rated degree) course and qualified as a heating, air conditioning and ventilation engineer and gained associate membership of the Institution of Heating and Ventilation Engineers (AMIHVE). After the required time to prove myself I was raised to a fellow (FIHVE). In the ensuing years the standing of this institution was elevated until it was granted a Royal Charter when the name was changed to the much more appropriate Chartered Institution of Building Service Engineers and I was transferred as a fellow (FCIBSE).

I was extremely lucky in that the company I joined was G.N. Haden & Sons Ltd. This firm was founded in 1816 by two brothers who had served their apprenticeships with James Watt. For most of my time at Hadens the Chairman was G.N. Haden himself, a direct descendant of the original founders. G.N., as he was known, was very much a member of the ruling class, the top people's old boy net. He lunched every day at The Athenium

Club with members of the Government and captains of industry. Hadens, the firm, was run on pre-war principles of straight dealing. They were scrupulously honest in their business activities and as a result of G.N.'s reputation and standing the firm got most of the prestigious contracts without competition throughout the 1950s until the rise of thrusting, not so honest competitive firms generated by the decline in national standards.

I was fortunate enough to be involved, albeit sometimes marginally, in some of these major projects. One of these was the Shell South Bank development on the site vacated after the Festival of Britain exhibition closed. This was by far the biggest building project of the time, the main contractors were Sir Robert MacAlpine and Sons, the biggest and toughest contractors in the country. Hadens were the Designing Contractors for the Building Services with a small office on the site. My involvement for a short period was in assisting in the design of the huge boiler plant. An interesting aspect of this was that the only practical boiler design was a German boiler type called Corner Tube. This easy to construct and virtually unrestricted size boiler originated when British bombers were destroying the German boiler plants and the factories they served faster than the Germans could replace them using conventional design boilers of that period. Hitler asked his advisors if there was anyone who could

Chapter 4

provide a solution and was told that there was such an engineer but that he was a Jew and he and his family were in a concentration camp, in effect condemned to die. Hitler ordered that the man concerned be taken from the camp and told that if he could design a boiler that could be built easily using materials generally available then he and his family would be released and their lives saved.

The result was the Corner Tube design. This boiler is entirely constructed using steel tubes and met the design criteria perfectly. I believe that, uncharacteristically, Hitler kept his promise and the designer survived the war only to die shortly afterwards from ruined health from his days in the camp. It was this design of boiler we chose for the Shell South Bank project where we had four of the largest built to that time.

I worked in Haden's Shell site office for a couple of months during this boiler house design.

The Shell Company used to make a lot of films of events in which they had an interest, using their own Shell Film Unit. They decided that they should have a film record of the construction of their Head Office, Shell South Bank, but as the construction time was several years they could not have their film unit tied up for so long and in consequence engaged a private film company based in Chelsea which consisted, as far as I know, of just one young man. I knew this chap slightly as he used to come into Hadens little canteen for tea and sometimes lunch and join us office lads for a chat. He stood out on the site among the several hundred navvies by having long hair. and wearing a plum coloured corduroy jacket with a yellow paisley cravat – very arty.

The initial stage of the building works consisted of excavating virtually the whole site for a depth of some 30ft plus to accommodate three levels of basements. This work involved the hire of virtually every tipper lorry in the South of England to take the excavated soil from the site down to fill in marshland on the North side of the Thames estuary.

The Bakerloo underground railway line passed through the North East corner of the site at a level well above the bottom of the site excavation. At one stage a station specifically for the Shell building was proposed but this was abandoned as it was too near to Waterloo to be practical. Anyway, the Bakerloo line underground railway certainly in this section is truly a tube, consisting of sections of steel tube just big enough to accommodate the train bolted together with flanges and containing the track and live rail. This tube was exposed as it emerged from the side of the site excavation in one corner and ran on a curve to exit a short distance away on the other side of the site. The Underground Railway people were most concerned as to the integrity of their tube for the passage of trains and so MacAlpines constructed a forest of scaffolding to support the

Chapter 4

exposed tube and carried out no excavation works in the area of the tube between 6 am and midnight, that is during the day when trains were running.

Furthermore to avoid straining the tube structure by exposing and excavating near it the nightly procedure was to slacken all the flange bolts on the sections of tube exposed in the excavations before starting work and re-tightening them in the morning before the first train. The night works were carried out under a battery of arc lights. Someone went into the tube tunnel during the night works and reported a fascinating picture of the curving tube tunnel lit at frequent intervals by thin shafts of light entering the tunnel through the slacked off flange joints. This was reported to the film chap who was asked to film this unusual picture.

I heard from the chap concerned what happened next. Apparently he checked and double checked with the Underground people at Waterloo Station that on the appointed night there would be no trains on the Bakerloo line after midnight and that the live rail would be switched off, the general station lights would be on and he would have access to the station platform and the track. This chap turned up at Waterloo Station carrying his camera, tripod and other gear, found all the required lights on, got down to the Bakerloo line by walking down stationary escalators all without seeing a soul. When down on the platform he could hear the noise of distant trains on other lines echoing up the tunnel. He walked to the end of the platform and climbed down into the tunnel instinctively avoiding the live rail and set off walking along the tunnel the few hundred yards to the location of the Shell excavation.

As he did so he was conscious that one of the distant train noises he had heard was becoming more distinct and then he noticed the rails vibrating slightly. "My God" he thought, "there is a train coming!!" He was too far into the tunnel to run back to the platform and there were no alcoves to shelter in as there are in some brick built tunnels and he knew the train was a relatively tight fit in the tunnel. With nothing else to do he pressed himself up against the side of the tunnel, chalk white, sweating profusely and praying fervently, only to be passed by a couple of workmen on a hand propelled maintenance trolley who just wished him "Goodnight" before disappearing round the bend.

It was an eye opener to me to see how MacAlpines ruthlessly overcame every difficulty that arose. During the excavation period the removal lorries took a lot of mud out onto the roads around the site which generated a complaint from Westminster City Council. Road sweeper lorries were made by Dennis at Guildford and in the 1950s these were only made to order on a two year delivery. MacAlpines visited Dennis

95

Chapter 4

and came back the same day with a new road sweeper signed and in the livery of the City of Oxford which continually patrolled the roads around the site for the year or so that the excavations took. They then cleaned it up and sold it direct to the City of Oxford.

When actual construction of the Shell buildings commenced MacAlpines constructed a concrete mixing plant in the middle of the site from which the correct mix of concrete was supplied to any part of the site through flexible hoses about twelve inch diameter using compressed air. The procedure was to pump the required quantity into the tube system at the mixing plant end – push in empty cement bags to form a plug and then connect the compressed air which blew the whole lot to the point where the concrete was to be placed. At the end of the delivery the tube was washed through with water and again some cement bags plugged the end of the tube and compressed air connected to blow the surplus back to the mixing plant where the end of the delivery tube was put into a skip which collected the waste rubbish.

One particular day a freelance sales representative, nothing whatever to do with the Shell site, was driving across Waterloo Bridge in his newly delivered Austin Westminster car, when it was hit broadside by what was obviously wet concrete and cement bags. The side windows and windscreen were broken and the bodywork damaged. The car was undriveable. The sales representative realised this salvo could only have come from the Shell site below and adjoining the bridge, he came to the site and after some difficulty in getting in, as by this time MacAlpines had a ten foot high close-boarded fence around the site, made contact with the MacAlpines senior man on site.

MacAlpines man with a labourer and dumper truck went out to look at the car, stationary on Waterloo Bridge, and accepted that it was their responsibility. They dragged the car back to the site, passed everything out of the car that the sales rep required that day and got a taxi from the rank at Waterloo Station with instructions to take the sales rep wherever he had to go that day and home in the evening, with the bill to them.

The sales rep went off complaining that he had waited eighteen months for his car and had only had it for a week. The following morning, before he left for work, the sales rep answered a knock at his front door at home to be met by a MacAlpine representative who handed him the keys to an exact match new Austin Westminster in the same colour and with all his knick-knacks in the car pockets standing at the kerb. How MacAlpines managed to jump the queue for this car was never explained.

A further lucky element of my time at Hadens was that I seemed to be appointed for any small and odd job that did not fit the normal pattern,

97

Chapter 4

whereas most of my contemporaries became involved in huge jobs which lasted two or three years. Jobs were allocated by Arthur Beardow, misnamed Chief Draughtsman, who was in charge of the Drawing Office and with whom I always got on very well.

One day Arthur Beardow called me into his office and said he had a bit of an odd job he would like me to do. This was a job in Dublin for which an Irish Consulting Engineer named Jacob had been appointed. Jacob was only a one man band and had neither the staff capacity nor technical know-how to design this complex and moderately sized job and had come to Hadens for them to design and specify the job for him and in return he would ensure that Hadens were appointed as the Sub-Contractor. I told Arthur Beardow that I would be pleased to take on this job.

I wrote to Jacob advising him of my involvement and he replied saying he would come to London so that we could get the project underway. Jacob duly turned up. He was only a few years older than me and arrived at our office in Tavistock Square in black jacket and waistcoat, striped trousers, with yellow string gloves, a rolled umbrella and a bowler hat. When I knew him better I asked him why he had dressed like that and was told that he thought all people in business in London dressed that way. He and I got on very well right from the start.

National Service and Hadens

Anyway, the job consisted primarily of a big and complicated air conditioning system for a large ballroom to be built as an extension to the Shelbourne Hotel, Dublin. The Shelbourne was, and possibly still is, the premier hotel in Ireland – equivalent to the British Ritz or Grosvenor House.

I and my lads got stuck into the design and specification for this project and ultimately prepared our price for the works which was duly accepted and agreed.

The project started physically by an inaugural Site Meeting being called and to be attended by everyone concerned so that the team could all meet each other. A very good idea not often followed at that time in England. I decided that I would go as a two day visit – one day for the Meeting the other to tie up the construction details. This would be the first time I had flown, other than a childhood adventure. Hadens were very good about this sort of thing. They booked the flights and hotel and dealt with everything else including an alarm call to my flat in Kensington Church Street where I was living at the time.

I flew out on the 8 am flight from London Airport by Aer Lingus who flew DC3S the civilian version of the wartime Dakota. This is a piston engined aircraft which, compared to modern planes made very heavy work of the whole thing. At take-off the plane waited at the end of the runway with the engine throttles wide open until the rivets in the wings were jumping, then the

Chapter 4

pilot took the handbrake off and the plane slowly gathered speed. You could see the trees at the ends of the gardens of the houses adjoining the airport getting closer and every time I did this flight I was convinced we would not get up in time. Eventually we seemed to just clear these trees and the roofs of the houses beyond and then start a laborious climb up to, I think, Liverpool, there at cruising altitude the engines would be throttled back and descent to Dublin would begin.

On this first trip the timing was tight. I was told that the 8 am flight landed some time before 10 am and I was to catch the airport bus to the Aer Lingus office in Dublin and walk the short distance to the Shelbourne Hotel arriving in good time for the 11 am meeting.

Everything went according to plan until we landed at Dublin where we came under the influence of the Irish way of doing things. The plane rolled to a standstill and the engines shut down on a beautiful sunny morning surrounded by long grass with lots of wild flowers and butterflies – and nothing happened. No cabin staff appeared, no exit door was opened. The passengers all just sat in their seats and did nothing. The only buildings in sight were what appeared to be ex-army Nissan huts about a quarter of a mile away, just visible in the shimmering sunshine. While looking in the direction of these huts I could gradually make out a man pushing a set of steps on wheels towards our plane. I thought he could not possibly be coming to let us out, but, after taking about twenty minutes, he did arrive and pushed the steps up to the fuselage. A stewardess appeared, opened the door and said we could disembark.

My programme had been seriously compromised by this delay, so with my small briefcase hand luggage I was quick off the plane, beaten only by one chap who obviously not only knew the form but was also late. I looked around for a bus to take us to the terminal and found none. The chap ahead had already set off walking fast through the grass towards the buildings in the distance, so I followed suit. I arrived, well ahead of the following passengers, hot and bothered, with my best suit covered in grass seeds, at the Customs Hall entry to Dublin Airport. This was a room about the size of a school hall with a row of trestle tables down one side behind which stood five men, the Customs Officers. Unfortunately it appeared they only had one uniform to share between them. One had the jacket on over normal civilian clothes, another the trousers worn beneath a fairisle pullover, a third had only the hat, the others merely had arm bands marked Customs.

I offered my bag but was told not to worry and directed to the exit at the far end of the room. From there it was a short way through those buildings to the main exit from the airport outside of which was a road round a roundabout with lay-

Chapter 4

bys in front of the entrance doors. There was no sign of the required bus into Dublin. The only member of airport staff was a chap sweeping the road. I went over and asked him where was the London flight bus into Dublin. He replied that the flight was late so the bus had left on time with no one on board. There were no taxis he told me but there was a normal service bus which passed the end of the hundred yard long airport approach road.

I went down to this marked bus stop, where I stood with several housewives with shopping for a short while until a bus came along. You paid the driver as you got on to the bus and I had to say that I needed to get to the Aer Lingus office – "That's OK" he said "we go right past and I will tell you when we get there". I then tendered a £1 note for the fare only to be told that the bus only took Irish money – which had never occurred to me and which I did not have.

"Not to worry," said the driver, "have this one on us".

The trip into Dublin was quite short and I alighted at the Aer Lingus office, which was actually just a large shop on the main street of Dublin. I checked the time – it was ten minutes past eleven, the Meeting was scheduled for eleven o'clock. I had blotted my copybook being late for this critically important Meeting.

With no time to walk to find the Shelbourne Hotel I went out to what was obviously a taxi rank in the middle of the wide road. These taxis were not like London black cabs but were beaten-up big American cars. I went to the first one – an old Ford V8, which appeared to be driver-less. As I walked past to go to the next one, a voice came out "where to Sir?" I said the Shelbourne Hotel, got in and expected the driver to sit up properly in his seat. But no – the driver was a tiny man whose head did not come above the seat back. We shot out into the traffic. Over the seat I could see the top of the steering wheel moving. The driver could only have been peering over the scuttle and window sills.

The Shelbourne Hotel turned out to be only a very short drive away. I rushed into the huge reception area staffed by porters and girl receptionists in brown uniforms and asked to be directed to the Site Meeting. Nobody knew anything about the Meeting. I suddenly had a dreadful feeling that I had got the day wrong and that all the drama of getting there had been a waste of time. Then one of the girls in Reception said – yes, there was a meeting in room something-or-other which was on the first floor. I raced up the stairs to the about twenty foot high first floor landing and found the room. It was by then about half past eleven. – I was seriously late. I gingerly opened one of the immensely tall doors to the Meeting Room expecting to find a Meeting in full swing – the room was empty. There was a long narrow table with a green baize cover and a

Chapter 4

huge Georgian silver coffee set and many unused coffee cups and a pair of very tall arched windows looking out over the leafy square outside.

I thought that perhaps the whole Meeting had gone to the site, which was part of the Shelbourne Hotel – but I did not know where. The only option I had was to wait in the room until they came back. I stood gazing out over the square worrying about the affect my lateness would have not only on this particular project but my engineering career generally. I had been like that for about five minutes when the doors opened noisily and a chap of about my age came in and said "You here for the Meeting? – I'm the Quantity Surveyor – would you look after this for me (his briefcase) I am off for a haircut" and with that he left.

Shortly after this further people arrived including my friend Jacob until by about twelve fifteen everyone, except the Architect, were there. I commented to Jacob that in England a Meeting at eleven o'clock started at eleven o'clock – he laughed and said "That's not the way we do it here."

The Architect then arrived so the Meeting could have started but he said it was too near lunchtime – so we would re-convene after lunch.

"Right," said Jacob "we'll get some lunch at the Bailey."

So off he and I went a short distance to what appeared to be a very rough pub. A gloomy and battered ground floor with a galvanized steel topped bar, which did not look at all promising. However, Jacob led the way to the first floor dining room which was a complete contrast, one big room with long tables and bench seats like a school dining room, but spotless table linen and silver cutlery. We were the only people in the dining room. Shortly a waiter in immaculate white shirt, black waistcoat with an ankle length white apron, offered us a menu on a piece of card measuring about two feet by three feet. Jacob waived this away saying to me that we do not need that – the Dublin Bay prawns are in and they're what we are having. So he ordered these and pints of draught Guinness.

The waiter reappeared with a wicker laundry basket filled with bread rolls which he placed on our table. He then brought another laundry basket filled with huge prawns and followed up with two pint glasses of Guinness. "Dig in" said Jacob, so I took about six prawns and a roll assuming that the prawns and rolls would be removed for some other customers. "No" said Jacob "these are all for us". Anyway for the next couple of hours we managed to make some impression on the prawn mountain while consuming a large amount of Guinness so that I don't remember much about our return to the Meeting which was over very quickly after everyone had been introduced to each other.

Jacob was very apologetic that he could not spend the evening with me as he had some prior

Chapter 4

engagement. However, he presented me with a ticket to a new Sean O'Casey play which had opened at the Abbey Theatre the night before and which had been the main topic of conversation among the members of the Site Meeting. So after a wash and brush up at my hotel, the only temperance hotel in Ireland into which Hadens had booked me, I set off to find the Abbey Theatre. It was close by and so I arrived very early. In going to my seat I passed through the bar, where I had a cup of coffee to fill in a bit of time, and was asked if I would like to order a drink for the interval which would be left ready for me so that I did not have to queue. A good idea I thought so I ordered half a pint of "brown" (ale).

Eventually the play started. It was all in Gaelic of which I could not understand a single word, but having a very simple plot I was able to roughly follow what was going on. When the interval of fifteen minutes came along I went to the Bar and located my half-pint glass of a brown liquid. At the first sip I knew it was not the brown ale I had been expecting. It was very strongly alcoholic but as the interval was short I guzzled away and managed to finish my drink in time. I do not remember much about the second half of the play – nor getting back to the hotel. The next morning I had a fearsome hangover which I explained to Jacob when I met him as arranged, and told him about my theatre trip and the extraordinary brown ale supplied in Dublin. He laughed and said that what I had got was a half pint of brown port; that is what you get if you ordered a "brown". In Ireland they do not have brown ale as in England. I had drunk quickly half a pint of brown port – hence the vicious hangover.

That first visit to the Shelbourne Hotel job was followed by several others during the course of the works on site which went very well to produce a very good final job. As mentioned at the outset this Shelbourne Hotel ballroom required air conditioning and the plant was designed to provide this amenity. It was also necessary that this air conditioning plant be silent in operation. By the technology of those days such silence could only be achieved using very slow speed centrifugal fans while the air quantities meant that these fans were very big – in fact the scroll casings stood about ten feet tall. As is the way of all building/engineering contracts final completion fell behind so that when the grand opening ball was fixed the air conditioning plant, although fully operational, had minor matters to be completed including guards on the four vee belt drives on the fans and final setting up of the system electric controls.

Everyone, including me, who had been involved with the project were invited to join the cream of Irish society and members of the Government at the opening Gala Ball. Hadens had a rule, with which I wholly agreed, that their staff would not be represented at opening balls, dinners and

Chapter 4

similar events. The reasoning behind this was that such invitations were normally addressed to one or more of the Directors who had had nothing to do with the job on a day-to-day basis. The people who designed and supervised the job – who deserved an invitation – were not usually included. Hence, the no acceptance rule. Of course Jacob had no such restriction and prepared for this ball by fitting himself out in full evening dress, white tie and tails.

What happened at the ball I got from newspaper reports and much later from Jacob himself.

The Ball was in full swing when the Architect, mixing with the top people, noticed that it was getting a bit warm and asked Jacob, as Consulting Engineer, to do something about it. This was a bit unfortunate as Jacob had had nothing to do with the design and very little to do with the installation, however he did know where the Plant Room was. So he took himself off there and located all the plant controls including temperature controls.

Jacob bent down to adjust the temperature controls for the air conditioning, which happened to be low down on the panel. In so doing the tails of his evening dress caught in the unguarded belts of the nearest fan. He was lifted off the ground and carried up to the top pulley and over the other side. This lifted Jacob well off the floor and dropped him down again when one of his tails tore off. Jacob cut his forehead in this drama, ruined his evening dress suit and got covered in the dust from a new, unsealed concrete floor. He made his way back to the Ballroom, dripping blood, to be hailed as the hero of the evening, praised in all the Dublin papers and on the radio. Jacob's professional career was made from this point onwards – he became Ireland's premier, perhaps only, Consulting Engineer for Building Services.

I remained in contact with Jacob after the Shelbourne Hotel and from this a couple of anecdotes arise. The first of these was that Jacob's office was one small room formed in the loft of one of the large four storey and basement Victorian houses in Dublin's professional district. Of course, this uninsulated little office was bitterly cold in winter. This was in the very early days of electric storage heaters which comprised concrete blocks with an electric heating element all contained in a metal case, and connected to an off-peak electric supply to heat up during the night and dissipate heat the following day. A salesman trying to sell storage heaters visited Jacob in an attempt to get these heaters specified for jobs which Jacob might do. To convince Jacob he presented him with a free issue heater for his own office. Jacob was duly grateful and put the heater into use.

Some months later Jacob arrived at his office one Monday morning to find it cordoned off with

Chapter 4

Police all over the place. Jacob was told that the Judges' Chambers on the ground floor had been bombed. Jacob explained that he had to get in as his office was on the top floor. When Jacob got to his office he found a hole in the floor with a broken electric flex hanging down in the place where the storage heater had been. Further investigation with the Police revealed that the heater had crashed through each floor below, making a bigger hole each time to end up, scarcely recognizable, in the basement. Bomb scare over – but Jacob had a lot of explaining to do.

Through Jacob, Hadens – that is me – were put in touch with the Irish Hospital Board who had a number of big hospitals for which the heating and hot water systems were served by big, inefficient hand fired boilers burning peat. The Board wanted efficient automatic boilers either by adaptation of existing boilers or replacement by modern oil fired boilers. I was looking forward to doing this job as it involved quite a lot of time going round Ireland surveying the existing boiler plants, but before the project got started it reached the ears of Max Priess a very excitable mid-European immigrant who ran Hadens small specialised Combustion Department and he made a big fuss saying that his group should deal with this essentially combustion matter. I saw his point and reluctantly accepted the Chief Draughtsman Arthur Beardows' decision to hand the job to Max Priess with me providing any technical back up required.

As I had nobody else in Hadens who knew anything about burning peat I had, through Jacob, got in contact with the very recently retired Chief Engineer of the Irish Hospital Board who was an acknowledged expert in matters of peat burning and whose name, I think, was Doyle. This chap had undertaken to give us all the help he could. I passed this information on to Max Priess who appointed one of his lads, John Grubb, to go and see Doyle. John Grubb was then probably thirty years old, unmarried and living with his widowed mother in Harrow. John Grubb had never been abroad or flown so I spent some time with him giving him a few tips and pointers and Hadens prepared his itinerary, got his tickets, etc. The retired engineer, Doyle, then lived in the very rural southernmost part of Ireland with a complete lack of hotels, so it was arranged that John Grubb would actually stay with Doyle for the three days of the visit. Anyway, on the appointed Monday morning off John Grubb went for his 8 am flight to Dublin and then a journey of, I think, four trains ending up with a tiny two carriage steam train to his destination. He was due back home on Thursday evening and back in the office on Friday morning.

I was busy with other things when, on the Friday morning, Haden's receptionist on the floor below mine telephoned asking me to go down to

Chapter 4

see a Mrs Grubb. This was John's mother who looked exactly like the Giles cartoon grandmother, complete with hat and hatpin. Mrs Grubb went for me demanding to know what I had done with her son who had not come home on Thursday evening as expected. I explained to Mrs Grubb that I had no knowledge of John's situation but I would make enquiries and keep her informed if she would go home and wait by the telephone. She accepted this and went off muttering dreadful threats of what she would do to me if anything happened to her son.

There was very little I could do – Doyle had no telephone. However, we did have a Dublin "office" actually only a labour depot run by a chap named Glasgow with whom I had had dealings during the Shelbourne Hotel job. I managed to contact Glasgow and asked him to make what enquiries he could. I had no information by the end of the day so I am ashamed to say I crept off home without contacting Mrs Grubb, praying that John would turn up during the weekend. On the Monday morning I rang Mrs Grubb to be told that John had arrived home on Sunday evening but he was most peculiar and was still in bed and would not be in the office before Tuesday. Later on the Monday morning I had a report from Glasgow who had pieced the whole thing together.

John Grubb had left home without breakfast very early to catch his 8 am flight to Dublin. The plane had no catering facilities. On arrival in

Dublin John had a rush to catch the first of his train connections and had taken all day to reach his final destination, without having had anything to eat. He was met at the tiny wayside station by Doyle with a pony and trap. At the first cottage they came to on leaving the station Doyle said "My sister lives here and would like to meet you" So in they went and were immediately offered a large glass of Irish Whiskey which John, not wishing to be rude and knowing no better, promptly drank. The journey resumed and after a few yards stopped at another cottage, this one owned by another relative, where John downed another large whiskey. This process continued through the village. John Grubb never remembered how many times.

Eventually they arrived at Doyle's house where his wife took pity on the then incoherent John Grubb who was unable to walk and said: "You poor dear – you must go straight to bed with a nice hot whiskey."

John Grubb was unconscious until midday the following day and awoke with a fearful hangover. "Right", said Mrs Doyle, "you must have a hot whiskey to set you up." After which, John Grubb passed back into unconsciousness. This repeated with occasional small quantities of food until the end of the week. Doyle knew that John Grubb was supposed to return home on the Thursday but he was not well enough. So Doyle and his wife went through John's things to find his return air ticket

Chapter 4

and contacted Aer Lingus for an alternative later flight at a suitable time. The only one available was late Sunday afternoon, this they booked.

John gradually improved as he became more acclimatised to a mainly whiskey diet so that by Sunday he could stand and walk but could not talk sensibly. The Doyles dressed him and gave him his bag, tied a big label on his lapel, saying "Please help me to flight xyz Dublin Airport" and put him on the train.

No small wonder that John was what his mother described as "peculiar" when he got home on the Sunday evening. He had learnt nothing about peat burning, however this did not matter much as not long after this visit the Irish Hospital Board discovered they were short of funds, the combustion revisions were postponed and I never heard any more about the project.

Another combustion story from Haden days comes to mind.

There was a firm called Gliksteins who had cornered the market for making flush panel doors used universally for the post war housing boom. Gliksteins were in the East End of London in Carpenters Row, the middle of the woodworking district. The door making produced very large quantities of sawdust for which there was very little use so its disposal was an expensive nuisance to Gliksteins. Gliksteins approached Hadens to see if we could devise a way of burning this sawdust in their boilers to save the cost of the oil they otherwise burnt. I was appointed for this job. I thought sawdust would be a super fuel and easy to burn. However this turned out to be incorrect. Sawdust just blankets the fire and smoulders or actually puts the fire out. I soon discovered that there was no sawdust burning equipment available on the UK market and for a while I was completely stumped.

Hadens had a very small periodicals library which contained publications from around the world. As a shot in the dark I had a look at the then current library contents and found, in a magazine, an article about equipment which, from the photographs, I thought was designed to burn a difficult fuel like sawdust. Unfortunately the leaflet was in German, which I do not read, so I passed it to Hadens translation man, a very senior engineer called Laurie Bull. Laurie Bull came back to me a couple of days later and said: "You're not going to like this but this equipment is the civilian version of the apparatus this firm designed and developed to incinerate the bodies of victims in the German concentration camps." I was doubly horrified not only for the origins of the equipment but also that Gliksteins were very much a Jewish firm and I said that I would have nothing whatever to do with it. I am not sure how my refusal, rather than the reason, got back to the directors but I was summoned to explain why I had mutinied and refused to consider something which would solve our clients' problem. I must

115

Chapter 4

add that in true Haden tradition when I had explained the position far from being censured I was congratulated and my status was elevated a little. I never solved the problem of how to burn Gliksteins sawdust.

I fitted in well at Hadens where I stayed for ten years and rose by luck to be the youngest group leader in the firm where there were some twenty groups among the hundred people in the drawing office.

Chapter 5 - Consulting

Some time after I joined Hadens, Peter Foreman left British Rail and started his own practice as a Consulting Engineer with offices in Pall Mall, London. He used to contact me about once a year asking me to join him. I resisted because I was happy at Hadens. Eventually, in 1962 Peter Foreman came to me and said he would like me to join him as an Associate Partner to open an office for him in Brighton with a full partnership, salary increase and a profit share if the office was a success.

This was most attractive, not least because I hated the train, tube and bus journey to and from Horsham to Hadens offices in Tavistock Square. So I left Hadens and went to Brighton.

Through his British Rail days Peter Foreman was a friend of Captain Ashley (reputedly Winston Churchill's pilot during the war) who leased part of the old Brighton railway works for his business of importing and assembling BMW Isetta bubble cars. Ashley allocated a couple of the rooms in the old railway works to me to start Foreman's Brighton office with one elderly draughtsman employee.

Peter Foreman got me in with Brighton Corporation who remained our major clients. The first job I did was Brighton's Police Headquarters

Chapter 5

followed by Brighton Law Courts. Over the years we also gained East Sussex County Council, Hampshire County Council and Hampshire Police Authority and several other private clients like the Hammerson Property Group. After about a year Peter Foreman bought a property in Hove into which I moved with the eight staff I then had.

As an aside, one of my abiding memories of this period, when we were in the offices in Hove, was on Friday 22 November 1963 when we heard that John F. Kennedy, President of the United States, had been assassinated.

By 1965 the Brighton office was making some £250,000 per annum profit but I had not received the promised salary increase or the full partnership. I was serving on the committee of South Holmes Housing Association in Horsham planning to develop some two hundred dwellings on the old Gillette Farm site in Roffey for which I was proposing a District Heating Scheme where space heating and hot water would be provided from a central boiler house – an economical and effective system. I suggested to Peter Foreman that if he gave me the promised salary increase and the full partnership I would get Foreman's Brighton office appointed as consulting engineers to this scheme in Roffey. He said he would if I came up to work in his London office. This I would not do – no more commuting to London – so I left Foreman & Partners and started my own practice of Colin Groves & Associates and got appointed as

Consulting

Consulting Engineer for the South Holmes development.

I helped my school friend John Warren convert the loft of Kingsway House, North Parade, Horsham into offices for himself as an architect and me with space in one corner. After a year we also took over the floor below where I had a couple of rooms for my office. Initially I employed Alan Church who had been a junior under me at Hadens and as work increased I took on a couple more people.

On the Committee of South Holmes Housing Association I met fellow member Leslie Keats, who was principal of a fair size London practice of Quantity Surveyors. I got on well with Les Keats from the outset. A few years older than I Les lived in Rusper with his wife June and Jane and I became firm social friends. Les introduced me to a long standing business associate of his, Architect Frank Lancaster, who was looking for a Consulting Engineer to form a team with him and Les for a biggish project for which he had just been appointed. This was an extension to the R and D Department and a new Head Office building for Colt (Ventilation) at Havant. Although he was a little older than me, Frank and I got on very well and on his recommendation Colts appointed me as Consulting Engineer for this project. This created a happy working team of chums who got on well and this led on to

119

Chapter 5

extensive social activities and lasted for many years.

Frank and Les were both successful in the London building world which had been unavailable to a little provincial Consulting Engineer like me. Frank, who had competed as a works driver in two Monte Carlo rallies, took a great interest in my motoring activities and when I first knew him was learning to fly a single engine Cessna light aircraft which he had just bought. Flying became his passion and he used to persuade me to go for pleasure trips after the site meetings at Colts. As time went on he progressed through various flying qualifications and bigger twin engine planes until he could fly day and night anywhere he wished. He and his wife used to fly down to the South of France for the weekend.

Entertaining clients and potential clients was always a problem for us professionals in those days when the rules of our Professional Institutions were much stricter than today. Most of the high level people Frank, Les and I dealt with were routinely taken out to lunch by people trying for their business and were very underwhelmed by such expensive activities. So under Frank's name we three joined the World Sporting Club sharing the costs between us. The World Sporting Club, a strongly Jewish organization with Jack Solomons the famous boxing promoter as Chairman, met at the Grosvenor House Hotel in

Consulting

Park Lane on a Sunday evening once a month for dinner and professional boxing matches.

Dining tables were set for eight which normally left two places after Frank, Les and I each with our own guest took our seats. Anyone could sit in these two places. We had film stars, television personalities, Members of Parliament and Cabinet Ministers and similar. Chatting to these people all evening impressed our guests mightily. The World Sporting Club was the best job-getting tool I ever came across.

Once a year the World Sporting Club had a Ladies Night when there was no boxing. This was a full on best dress and family jewels outing which our little group went to with our wives who enjoyed it immensely. The whole set up was very up-market as evidenced when the evening finished at 1a.m. on the Monday morning. Park Lane outside the Grosvenor House would be completely blocked by private chauffeur driven Rolls Royces to take everyone, except us of course, home. I very much enjoyed The World Sporting Club where I mixed with the cream of London stage, screen and business society on equal terms. It was here that I learnt how to distinguish between true celebrities and jumped up, media created, non celebrities. Never be over-awed by a celebrity. Just think of them sitting on the toilet with their pants round their ankles. This will get everything into perspective.

Chapter 5

To return to establishing my own practice, the lease John Warren had on the offices ran out after five years and the landlord, John King, got difficult about him subletting to me, so I decided to get my own offices. At this time Jane's parents lived in 42 North Street, Horsham which was a medieval timbered building and they wanted to sell to move to Bracknell, I cannot remember why but I offered to buy the property provided I could get planning permission to convert to offices. After many delays Jane's parents could wait no longer and sold the house. I then found a little cottage known as Westlands Cottage in Foundry Lane, Horsham which was an unmade unadopted road near Horsham station. This I bought freehold. I got planning permission to convert Westlands Cottage, renamed Grove House, to offices which I did. This little cottage had been built in 1900 as the chauffeur's house and car garage at the end of the garden of Westlands House, which stood in Kings Road. I moved Colin Groves and Associates into Grove House in 1970.

The owner of Westlands House was named Norris who was a rather pompous partner in a big London consulting engineers practice who thought he should patronise me. Jane and I were invited to tea one Sunday. While eating cucumber sandwiches on the terrace at the back of Westlands the subject of the possibility of the future sale of Westlands came up. Norris said that it was such a valuable site for redevelopment that he would sell it at so much a square foot and that the costs would be way beyond a little fellow like me.

About a year later there appeared on my gatepost a notice of planning application made by Lintotts, the engineers then on the old foundry site, for converting the garden of Westlands to a car park and the house into an apprentice hostel. In order to do this they would have to make a vehicle access across my land at the front of Grove House. They had not approached me in this matter. I made an objection to the Council and the planning application was refused.

As it was apparent that Norris was selling Westlands I wrote to him and asked if he would consider an offer from me. I had no reply. Some weeks later I had a telephone call from an independent local estate agent named Dicken whom I knew socially, who asked if he could come and see me. I agreed and he came to my office with a chap from Knight Frank & Rutley, upmarket agents in London. He was very embarrassed but eventually said Norris had asked him to come and sound me out as to what I would be prepared to offer for Westlands. Having rather lost interest I said I was only interested in it as a house to live in, not for redevelopment, and for that I would offer £45,000. Dicken said Norris was looking for at least £500,000 so the interview terminated.

Chapter 5

Over the ensuing months we occasionally saw people looking at Westlands, but it did not sell, perhaps because the housing market was depressed. Then Dicken took to telephoning me roughly monthly, initially saying Norris would consider an offer of £400,000, then £300,000 and then £200,000 and then eventually Dicken came to my office and asked would I pay £100,000 for Westlands. When I said no, Dicken said he must talk to Norris and he telephoned me about an hour later and said Norris would accept my original offer of £45,000. I replied that since then the market had gone down further and my offer was now £40,000. Dicken then negotiated up to £42,000 at which price I bought Westlands.

Having bought Westlands I split off the bottom of the site beside my office in Foundry Lane into my firms name, Colin Groves & Associates, and applied for planning permission for two three storey offices each nominally three thousand square feet floor area. One office was linked to my office cottage and its mirror image the other office, making a terrace of three interlinked units. The new offices were designed in Georgian style compatible with the original cottage surrounded by an off road car park and all in a garden setting to make what I thought an attractive ambiance for professional offices. The planning office agreed with me and planning permission was granted unconditionally.

Consulting

I set to, largely on my own, but with occasional help from the lads in the office and direct subcontract labour to build both offices up to two stories with a temporary roof, as this was all I could afford at the time. The original cottage became Number 1 Grove House whilst the new extension offices became numbers 2 and 3 respectively. Upon completion I let both buildings on five year leases, one to Japanese desalination engineers and the other to a firm of Quantity Surveyors. At the end of those initial leases the Japanese firm went away and the Quantity Surveyor moved into No 1, the Cottage, which I vacated to move into one floor of the extension offices so that I could fit out my big aluminium yacht in the car park adjoining the offices. Eventually I built the second floor to the whole of the office buildings and I then moved my firm back into the cottage and let No 2 to the Royal Mail and the other to The Born Free Foundation – headed by Virginia McKenna whom I had played tennis against when I was at school.

I had for some time planned on retiring at about fifty five years old, not to sit around waiting to die but to pursue some other interests and a different way of life. Hence, the idea behind the big aluminium boat, details of which appear elsewhere, was to have a boat to retire on and to do some extended worldwide cruising.

Chapter 5

Photo 1: Grove House

Over the preceding years I had several associates each of whom I was intending to make full partners to take over the firm when I retired. The first of these was Alan Church who had a ruthlessly ambitious wife who persuaded Alan to leave me and take a position as managing director of C A Goodwin Ltd the local heating engineering contractors who my firm had lifted from a small plumbing firm to a fair sized provincial contractor. Not only treacherous but unwise as Alan only lasted about a year until the firm closed down. Next was Peter McLean who did not enjoy driving from Burgess Hill to Horsham every day and was head hunted by a consulting engineer with a promise of immediate partnership who started up in Burgess Hill a couple of minutes from Peter's house. I do not think the partnership ever materialised and this practice folded up a couple of years later and I lost touch with Peter.

Finally there was Derek Bentley who was with me for many years. Derek, also from Burgess Hill, was unmarried and lived a very sheltered life with his mother. I liked Derek and went to a good deal of trouble to raise his ambitions from a subordinate to an executive so that he could take over from me. Unfortunately, psychologically Derek was unable to make that transition which all came to a head when I arranged for him to take the junior partner in one of our most important architect clients out for Christmas lunch. Derek knew him very well as they had worked together for over a year on the extensions to Collyers School, my old school, in Hurst Road, Horsham, but Derek failed to do this because the architect's car was off the road and Derek was too embarrassed to offer his very rough fibreglass Rochdale Olympic car and never thought of ordering a taxi. When we discussed this debacle Derek said, using his words, that he was perfectly happy being an Indian and he didn't want to be a Chief. This revelation put my retirement plans into jeopardy.

At about this time at a new friend's Christmas party I met a chap about ten years younger than me who said he had set up as a Consulting Engineer in Horsham. I mentioned my intended

Chapter 5

imminent retirement and he said he might be interested in buying my practice.

At this point I made the worst error of commercial judgement of my entire professional career coupled with my worst ever judgement of human character. The chap concerned had no money so he took over my firm with me on a five year contract as part-time consultant and with a 40 per cent share of the profits. For the first couple of years things went relatively well except it transpired that my associate's only attribute was that he managed to get us appointed for lots of jobs – but as an engineer and designer he had no aptitude at all, so I worked full time and ran the office with an increasing number of staff, ending up with fourteen engineers and draughtsmen.

The firm made a lot of money and this went to my colleague's head. He left his wife and two children and started an affair with the wife of a senior executive in Sun Alliance head office in Horsham. This was none of my business until the firm's yearly accounts revealed that he had spent something over £20,000 on gifts and weekends away with his mistress and had tried to conceal this money as firm's expenses, thereby reducing the profit of which 40% was due to me. When I approached him in this matter he replied that it was his firm and he would do what he liked.

Shortly after this, before anything had been resolved, his affair ended when late one evening the woman's husband caught the two of them in a very compromising situation in my office car park. My associate moved out lock, stock and barrel over the Christmas office shutdown. I sued for compensation due to breach of contract. In the way of litigation this took five years to be resolved in the High Court but when I won I was awarded over a quarter of a million pounds damages and won the costs. My associate promptly went bankrupt so I got nothing and had to pay my own costs.

Not a very good way to end ones professional career. However, this experience did reinforce what I had known for a long time which is – stay away from litigation from which the only people to make money are the solicitors and perhaps expert witnesses.

One last point I find of interest is that all the foregoing occurred when my black German Shepherd bitch, Bella, spent all day in my office with me. She was friends with all the staff except for this associate. He used to make a great fuss of the dog but she ignored him. She never bit him but as I knew her so well, I could tell there were times when she was on the verge of so doing. She knew from the outset that the man was a crook and not to be trusted. I only wish I had been able to recognize this at the outset. The Law in the matter of bankruptcy is seriously flawed. I am told that my erstwhile associate changed the name of the firm and carried on in business without any apparent difficulty while I got nothing.

Chapter 5

In reviewing my career as an engineer I am immensely grateful to the Army for recognising my latent talents. I cannot think of any other career which could have possibly provided the enthusiasm and satisfaction of engineering. I am unable to understand why engineers are not more highly regarded in Britain, whereas elsewhere they are held in the highest esteem and rank among the top professionals. In Britain we do not acknowledge that engineers enable every part of our lives to function. Everything, except possibly art, is the product of an engineer's imagination and technical skills. I, in my small way, contributed to that.

I was involved in some very prestigious building projects, initially through Haden's standing, then through Peter Foreman's wheeling and dealing and latterly by my own reputation and competence. It has always given me a great feeling of achievement to pass a building the services of which I designed. A semi-permanent legacy to the world, I suppose.

It would not be appropriate to list all of even the more prestigious projects but I may mention, firstly from the Haden days – the boiler plant of the Shell building on the South Bank, the final phase of Guildford Cathedral, completion of the external steam and condense mains at AWRE Aldermaston, and my design of a circular all glass boiler house on the cliff top at the Lyle & Scott factory, Dunfermline, Scotland where to my great pleasure it became a maritime navigational mark entered on the Admiralty Chart as such, and the air conditioning for a new ballroom in the Shelbourne Hotel, Dublin.

Then while running the autonomous Brighton office for Foreman & Partners, Brighton Police Headquarters, Brighton Law Courts, Hampshire Police Headquarters, and several Brighton area Schools.

Finally as Colin Groves & Associates, South Holmes, Roffey, Horsham the development of some three hundred dwellings ranging from flats to detached bungalows and an old peoples home with the first district heating scheme which stood on its own feet financially. It proved so cheap to operate that charging tenants on heat meter readings as originally designed produced too little income and a flat charge was introduced. The publicity from that successful project caused me to write a paper for presentation at the District Heating Association, which in turn led to my designing a district heating scheme for a development of some large detached prestigious houses in Amman in Jordan. For a short time I had an office in Amman.

The Churchill Housing Estate, Lancing, Sussex was a smaller but successful district heating scheme, which demonstrated that such schemes did not have to be very big to be economically viable.

Chapter 5

Perhaps my most prestigious project was Worth Abbey Church, at Worth Abbey in East Sussex. The planning for this development had started in 1933 and came to fruition in the 1970s. The Architects were Brett & Pollen, Brett was Viscount Esher, then President of the RIBA.

The basically square single space building had a funnel shaped ramped floor. Based on my much earlier experience with Guildford Cathedral I knew that the correct way to heat such a large open and high building was by radiant heating from embedded floor panels, normally considered feasible only for flat horizontal floors. By a good deal of design time I came up with a system of small bore copper floor panel pipes each of which was confined to one contour of the floor. With a good deal of trouble from the installing contractor the floor panels were provided exactly to my design and the system worked and continues to work perfectly. I also designed and had constructed from mild steel large bore water pipe aged on completion, some medieval style light fittings for the church as the architect could not find a style of lighting he considered appropriate in spite of a worldwide search.

My firm was retained as consulting engineers by West Sussex County Council for some twelve years during which time we acted for some two hundred projects both large and small.

Finally, the last major project I did was the Joint Credit Card Company Headquarters at

Consulting

Basildon in Essex. This organization processed all credit cards issued by any bank, building society and similar with the exception of, I think, only one bank which might have been Lloyds. For this very large new build office complex we did all the services e.g. heating, air conditioning, ventilation, hot and cold water supplies, drainage, all electrical services including lighting and lifts. The value of these services in 1980 amounted to nearly two million pounds.

A sideline to my practice was that I personally became in demand as an Expert Witness in legal proceedings when mechanical and or electrical services were involved. This work started when I acted for Lord Camden in connection with his London mews flat. Word must have spread because thereafter we were retained by a very large firm of solicitors in Lincolns Inn Fields in London and subsequently asked by other solicitors in London and Brighton. Not only did this work pay well but I enjoyed it because I was part of the legal processes to which the public were not privy. A lot of work was done late into the night in the Wig & Pen Club in The Strand in London.

There were a couple of ancillary matters during the development of my own practice. When I first started my only commission was the district heating scheme at South Holmes, Roffey. I and my one staff, Alan Church, had to work on this

Chapter 5

project for eighteen months before I got any fee income.

This period was an enormous strain for me so I had to raise money from every source, including my mother-in-law, to pay wages, office expenses and feed the family.

To obtain some income I taught Building Services to students at Crawley College on one day each week. This, my first inside experience of teaching, was an eye opener. The head of the building department was a little Welshman completely devoid of any charisma or authority as his whole aim was not to upset his bosses in County Hall. I disturbed the smooth passage of his life very early on. The people in my class were all day release students sent by building firms in the Crawley area. With one exception they were reasonably interested in the subject. The exception was much better dressed than all the others and was the son of the owner of a major building firm in the area who saw no point in the class as he would take over his father's firm in any case. This lad had a sycophantic side-kick who followed him in all things.

At my first class everything went well until lunchtime. When the class restarted after lunch at 2pm the exception and his mate were not there but came in noisily to disrupt the class at about 2.15. I asked them why they were late and was told they had got held up. The following week the same thing happened, these two were not there at

2pm start after lunch. They came in at about 2.20 and I kicked them out of the class telling them that if they could not attend on time I did not want them in the class at all. The exception got very indignant and said he would tell his father who was a Governor of the College and that I would be out on my ear. I left him and his chum standing in the corridor outside the classroom. At the end of the lesson, the Head of Department, the Welshman, was waiting outside to speak to me. He said I could not kick out the son of the Governor as I had. The father would be down here and unless I apologised heads, I think he meant his, would roll. I told him I would not be apologizing to anyone. The next week the exception and his chum were in class promptly after lunch and I never had any more trouble from this lad for the remainder of the year.

In the late 1960s we were involved in many Local Authority housing schemes, financed by Central Government in an attempt to overcome the chronic shortage of low cost rented accommodation. The very tight cost constraints meant that all such accommodation was built as small and cheaply as possible. To prevent size and cost being reduced to an impractical and unacceptable degree the Government issued the 'Parker Morris' rules which set out the minimum size for every room and other features which were considered essential. One room given very little space (or indeed thought) by Parker Morris was

Chapter 5

the bathroom which had to have a normal size bath, a wash hand basin and a WC, being mechanically ventilated if it did not have an opening outside window. From my point of view the design of the services for these bathrooms presented some insurmountable problems, the bathrooms had to be heated in the winter and had to have some means of airing towels. In the normal course of events these requirements were easily met by a radiator on the heating circuit for heating and a heated towel rail from the hot water service primary for year round service. The problem was that one of these appliances operated at mean boiler water temperature of some 170°F (76°C), and the other at only slightly less. The very constricted space in these bathrooms meant that it was almost impossible to avoid touching either the radiator or towel rail when towelling off after a bath with the resultant painful burn, this was particularly true for children.

I decided the answer was to provide the same amount of heat but from an extended low temperature source rather than a small high temperature one. I invented and patented a device named BATHRAD. This comprised a heating element formed from one inch square mild steel tube in an oblong shape with a middle rail which was clipped in contact with a zintex coated mild steel sheet bath panel surfaced with a selection of decorative plastic finishes. The device was fed from the space heating (radiator) circuit and worked by the heat generated by the element, equivalent to that of a radiator, being transmitted to the bath panel by conduction. The larger surface area of the panel dissipated the heat over a large area which itself did not have a high temperature to the touch due to the plastic surface coating.

A full UK patent number 1204751 dated January 1968 for this BATHRAD was obtained initially in its water form and subsequently in an electrically powered mark II unit developed by public interest. I built a number of prototype BATHRADS and fitted one to the bath of Severals House where we lived at that time.

BATHRAD worked far better than I had anticipated, it more than adequately heated the bathroom and towels hung over the side of the bath dried to crisp fluffiness, but two other unexpected benefits were apparent. The first was that the bath structure was permanently warm and so when you ran a bath you needed less hot water and when you got in the bath the surface was warm to the bottom. The second was that after bathing a grubby child or indeed a grubby adult and draining the dirty water away there was no rush or difficulty in removing the tidemark around the bath, which stayed warm and residues were easy to remove.

So my invention was a success, all I needed was someone to make and market it.

Chapter 5

During the late 1960s my father had retired from British Rail Southern Region and had a part time job keeping the accounts for Horsham Precision Engineering Ltd (HPE) a firm owned by Peter Ryman and with a small factory in Blatchford Road, Horsham. HPE had grown as a subcontract precision machinists to several large manufacturing firms who over the previous year or so had taken their machining in-house. HPE's fall in business had reduced the previous staff level of fifteen to one, the foreman, and Peter Ryman was desperate to find something to keep his factory going.

My father mentioned BATHRAD to Peter Ryman who jumped at the chance of being involved. Peter Ryman and I formed BATHRAD Ltd as equal shareholders and directors. Peter Ryman was a very clever hands-on engineer and quickly developed the machinery and equipment to mass produce BATHRAD.

At this point a fundamental flaw in our strategy was introduced.

Based on the saying "If you invent a better mousetrap, the world will beat a path to your door" we decided to market BATHRAD ourselves although neither I nor Peter Ryman had any sales experience. Furthermore, I was in a difficult position professionally as the strict rules of the Association of Consulting Engineers, the professional body to which I had to belong in order to practice, current at that time, expressly forbade a member being involved in any associated trade.

Photo 2: Bathrad Leaflet

So marketing was down to Peter Ryman with me assisting anonymously in the background. After fixing a very reasonable price for BATHRAD we tested the ground with a stand at EXPO, a county show at Ardingly. We handed out many leaflets but did not obtain one sale.

Chapter 5

Next we felt we needed to get at a potentially bigger market and so we took a stand for two consecutive years at the Ideal Home Exhibition at Earls Court, London. Here again there was a lot of interest and we handed out thousands of leaflets but obtained no measurable sales.

After the Ideal Home show Peter Ryman, who was actually very shy, realised that he was not good at dealing with the public face to face and against my wishes engaged a freelance sales representative. This chap's name I do not recall but I remember him being festooned in gold rings, chains and watches, etc and he was very much a 'Flash Harry' who achieved very little.

I managed to pressurize Peter into calling at some major potential clients with some success. We sold some thousand BATHRADS to Battersea Council for their extensive development of council flats and had similar but smaller success with other Councils. But it was an uphill struggle and after a few years Peter Ryman decided to sell his factory and cease production of BATHRAD. This was a sad end to a device which I am still convinced had unlimited potential which would have made me a multi millionaire several times over had we sold to a major sales concern as I had wanted to do initially.

I should have learnt from a project some years earlier, that inventing something is all very fine but you must find a proper organization to market it. Trying to do this yourself is doomed to failure.

Consulting

Long before BATHRAD, an MP called Gerald Nabarro started and pursued a campaign with grants to have the thermal insulation of roofs of industrial buildings and factories improved to reduce heat loss and hence energy waste. This was the then unrecognised start of the current energy saving campaign and was very necessary, as most industrial building and factory roofs were single skin corrugated asbestos cement sheeting.

A number of firms started to advertise that they would apply insulation materials under asbestos roofing. I did not think that was the way forward primarily because it left the brittle and weak asbestos cement sheets in place which would perpetuate the frequent deaths and injuries resulting from people walking on and falling through these asbestos cement roofs as they were not capable of carrying a man's weight.

I set about designing a light load-bearing thermal insulating roof sheeting to replace asbestos cement of the same sizes so that is could be carried on the existing roof structure without alteration.

I decided on a stressed skin construction. Because I was involved with aluminium roof sheeting for Severals House, mentioned elsewhere, I settled on dimpled aluminium sheet for the upper outer skin and pre-decorated hardboard for the inner skin bonded together with some fifty millimetres of rigid polyurethane foam, which I knew could be formulated to provide the required

Chapter 5

tensile strength while giving high thermal insulation. With a couple of chums we built the very strong and heavy mould required due to the high pressure generated by the polyurethane activated liquid poured into the mould to foam up and bond. After a good deal of experimentation we produced roofing panels fully up to expectations and more than able to meet the design requirements. For many months I tried to get manufacturing and marketing firms interested without success until in the end I got engrossed in other things and shelved the roof panel project. If you do not get the marketing arrangements properly sorted out at an early stage your project will not succeed.

I must have been in an inventive mood at this period. I was asked by an architect chum to help him submit an entry for an international competition for the design of standard army camps for the Turkish Army. The prize was £100,000 and international fame. These camps were to be constructed using factory built prefabricated items. We already had a proven system of easily assembled standard building components, the SCOLA System used for new school building on which to base the building design.

There was a need for space heating and domestic hot water which could be satisfied by a straightforward UK style district heating scheme simplified and cheapened by having the distribution pipework above ground, acceptable in a utilitarian development like an army camp.

However, there was one other amenity requirement not so easily or cheaply achieved – this was for comfort cooling for particularly the many relatively small residential huts. Full air conditioning by either central plants or room conditioners was not warranted and would have been very expensive. Something simple was required.

I dreamed up a system of two layer aluminium pitched roofs. The under layer of aluminium sheet was the actual water tight membrane while the outer layer of aluminium sheet was spaced off some 100mm and was open at the ridge and eaves. Cold water was pumped to a perforated pipe at the ridge to produce a film of water down the inner skin to exit to a gutter at the bottom and back for recirculation. Ambient hot outside air passed between the sheets by natural convection to produce evaporative cooling of the water film and hence the inner roof membrane. In winter the water would be drained and dampers used to close the ridge and eaves openings to produce an air space insulated roof.

We did not win the competition, it was won by an American consortium with a very ordinary design but I suspect a political and financial aid carrot may have introduced.

Chapter 6 - Influences

When I was about sixteen I was introduced to elfin Anne Rowland who was a cousin of my friend Johnny Hull. Anne was my age, was at Horsham High School for Girls and lived with her mother in a second floor flat above Russell & Bromley shoe shop in West Street, Horsham. Anne became my permanent girlfriend for the next eight years or so and although I behaved very badly and had many other liaisons during that period I always went back to Anne in the end.

Together we learnt all about sex, being quite convinced that we had invented it. Sometime after my National Service Anne and I became engaged to be married, I cannot now recall what prompted such a drastic step, probably me trying to put right some transgression. I now cannot remember which of us broke off our engagement, probably Anne fed up with me. After Anne Rowland, I continued my lothario ways but my life was regulated by commuting to and from London every day, which produced some interesting side effects. I used to travel with train friends in the buffet car on the way up in the mornings and in the same carriage on the way home in the evenings.

One commuting friend was named Tristram and he travelled from Bognor every day. Now

Influences

Tristram was not conventionally handsome as he had a broken nose, but he did have charm and charisma and an Allard J2X exotic red sports car. He had incredible success with girls. Two seductions each weekend was his norm.

I pressed him for the secret of his success and he eventually let me into his secret – it was Merrydown Cider (the original version). Merrydown Cider came from a farm near Horam in East Sussex bought by a demobilized, I think, Major, after the War purely as a house for his family to live in. Adjoining the house was an apple orchard which produced inedible apples. The Major mentioned this down in his local pub and was told that his apples were cider apples and that his farm had been a major brewer of cider in years gone by. The publican pointed out an elderly regular who had worked at the farm before the War. The Major persuaded the old employee to come back to the farm and direct the resurrection of the old equipment still in the barn and help make some cider. This they successfully did and made much more cider than their family could consume so gave bottles to all their friends – all of whom said how good it was – and why did they not sell it to the public.

The Major supplied Merrydown to two hotels, the Downs at Hassocks and the Norfolk in Bognor.

Tristram used to pick up his girl of the moment in the Allard and take her to the Norfolk and offer

Chapter 6

a drink, which she would decline as her mother had told her not to drink. Tristram would then say, well have a cider that's almost like lemonade. Oh yes would say the girl and she would get a Merrydown, then sold in half or one pint tankards like beer. Half a pint of Merrydown and Tristram had his evil way.

Following this revelation, Bet Spratt, Keith Gray and I and my girl of the moment used to go to the Downs at Hassocks fairly regularly for their very simple 'dinner dance' on a Saturday night and we used to drink Merrydown with great success. It was very strong.

Some little while later, during a heat wave, a teetotal clerk in the Licensing Office and his wife were on holiday in Bognor. Out for a walk they got thirsty and called in at the Norfolk for a drink. The wife had a lemonade, but the husband, on holiday, had a pint of cider, Merrydown. He had only drunk some of his cider when his legs gave out and he had to go back to his bed and breakfast by taxi to sleep it off.

True to his calling he informed his office of this 'cider' called Merrydown being sold in the Norfolk. The resultant inspection found that Merrydown had the same percentage of alcohol as whiskey or gin. It was withdrawn from sale at the Norfolk and the Downs and had to be remarketed in a diluted form in small bottles at a much higher price due to the duty levied.

Merrydown has continued to be produced and is widely sold in a much diluted form.

Another of these travelling companions was a small chap named Harold Hobbs a little bit older than me who was a solicitor and always very well dressed except for an occasional raglan raincoat which was very tatty and most unlike Harold. One evening I was early for the train at Victoria having been to a site nearby. The train was in the station and walking down the almost empty platform ahead of me was Harold Hobbs in his tatty raincoat. When he got to our carriage he stopped, looked up and down the platform and then picked up the front of his coat hooked it onto something on the carriage door and then jerked it away. He came walking back up the platform and when he got to me I asked him where he was going "Look at this" he said pointing to a tear in the front of his raincoat, "I'm off to see the ticket inspector".

When he joined me in our carriage I asked him what had been going on. He said "I needed a new raincoat and now British Rail will buy me one. I get most of my clothes this way."

I was most impressed and said tell me how you do it. He said the coat on the nail was straightforward, as I had just seen. But more usual and lucrative was a defect in a product. For example, if you found a black man's finger in your tin of corned beef there was a set pattern to obtain compensation. First you write to the manufacturers setting out your complaint. They

Chapter 6

will reply saying it is impossible but if you send the tin and the finger they will look into it. Do not comply, never let the evidence out of your possession. If you send the evidence the manufacturer will say that this could never have happened in their factory and they have disposed of the items you sent. That will be the end of the affair. You retain the evidence and say to the manufacturers they have a week to inspect it before you go to the Public Health people. This will probably result in a free offer of a year's supply of corned beef. You turn this down and it will be replaced by a cash offer, which will be progressively increased until you accept, but do not get too greedy otherwise you will kill the thing off and get nowhere.

A couple of weeks later Harold Hobbs appeared wearing a brand new very expensive looking riding raincoat, very smart it was too.

Some months later Jane had bought a fruit malt loaf of bread. I was cutting slices for tea when I found embedded in the loaf the unmistakable end of a broken milk bottle. Hooray, I said to Jane here we have a nice little earner to ease our perpetual money shortages. I wrote to the makers of the malted loaf at their factory at Three Bridges as suggested by Harold Hobbs. They replied exactly as he said they would. I replied refusing to send the evidence but offering their inspection before I got onto the Public Health people. I never had any reply to that letter. I went to see the Public Health office and was told that they really weren't very interested. The evidence stayed in our kitchen for a month or more and became so dried up and shrunken that the milk bottle part just fell out so we had to throw it away.

Harold Hobbs had married Jill Berkley-Barton, a girl on the fringe of our Horsham social scene and they lived in a very nice unusual stone built house in Guildford Road, Horsham eventually with their children. Some years after the raincoat on the train incident Harold Hobbs died suddenly. This left Jill in financial straits as it became apparent that Harold was not as well off as everyone had thought. Anyway Jill managed to carry on in somewhat reduced circumstances. Some years later the Antiques Roadshow went to Horsham and Jill's son, then a teenager, said to his mother, why don't we take along some of the small items of silverware that his father Harold had collected for some years. So Jill and her son took a selection of these silver items to the Antiques Roadshow, which Jane and I watched, primarily because it was at Horsham.

When Jill spread out these pieces on the table the expert nearly had apoplexy. Every one was a unique high quality item and from Jill's description of the whole collection he valued it at several hundred thousand pounds. This was in the 1980s. As advised Jill put the whole lot on the market and did realise the suggested amount. The

Chapter 6

end of her money problems. Harold was a canny little man.

While unsuccessful with the broken milk bottle in the malt bread, I had been somewhat more successful some years earlier. Before I was married when I was still living with my parents I became involved in a Haden job of providing three enormous new air compressors to the Gillette Industries factory on the Great West Road, London. Gillette manufactured every sort of razorblade under their own and other names, the only exception being Wilkinson-Sword blades. The job involved gutting an existing building and installing three compressors. There was only one company who made compressors this big and this was Sulzers in Switzerland and their compressors were on an eighteen-month delivery, so I started the job by designing alterations to the stripped out compressor house, then the compressor bases, floor ducting, etc and overseeing these building works. This involved going up to Gillette's in a firm's car to see the Works Director, whose name was Woodgate, the client representative. These visits were very frequent and during this time I got on very well with this Woodgate, who was not very much older than me. Then there was a lull while we awaited the new compressors from Switzerland.

At this time I was shaving with a normal Gillette razor using 'blue' blades bought in packets of five at a relatively high price. One

Influences

Saturday I was in the Market in Horsham and there was a trader operating a 'Dutch' auction where he starts off at a high price and brings it down in stages to a very low price to sell the first of a line. This trader was a regular who normally sold tea towels and tablecloths, etc but this Saturday he had packs of twenty by five 'blue' Gillette razorblades which he knocked down to I think ten shillings (50p), an offer I could not refuse so I bought a packet.

A few days later having emptied the blade pack I had been using, I opened my new bumper pack and got out a packet of five blades, unwrapped one and put it in my razor. I took repeated strokes down the side of my face without any effect. I rinsed the shaving foam off, had a look at the razor to find that, by good chance, the side I had been using there was no blade projecting, while on the other side the blade was sticking out clear of the razor by about an eighth of an inch. I opened the razor and found the locating hole punchings in the blade were not in the middle as they should have been but very much off centre. I opened one or two other packs of blades and found they were all the same.

I shaved with the old blade and had to rush off to catch the train to go to work. Inspection the following evening revealed that all the blades I had bought in the Market were similarly defective. This was not quite the disaster it could have been because in Hadens drawing office we drew in ink

Chapter 6

on tracing paper. To erase ink on tracing paper you scratch out the ink with a sharp razorblade. Unfortunately the office was supplied by members of staff bringing in used and therefore dull blades, which did not work very well. I was able to supply brand new sharp blades to all and sundry. I was very popular. In the meantime being a bit fed up with failing to find cheap razorblades I bought a Phillips electric razor.

The next time I went to Gillette's over lunch I told Woodgate about my offset Gillette razorblades. He laughed and said it was a good story but it could not possibly happen with their very strict quality control.

For the following visit I took a couple of unopened packs of five defective blades and gave them to Woodgate to open. He did so and almost fainted when he saw the offset stamping. "Wait here" he said, "I must show this to our Chairman, who happens to be in today." He returned a few minutes later and thanked me for bringing these defective blades to his attention. They would look into it.

A few weeks later I went to Gillette's again and at the gate the security guard said "Mr Groves the Chairman would like to see you, so park next to his Rolls Royce in the Directors' car park and go straight up to see him". The Chairman, Lord something or other, greeted me effusively and said that they had effectively traced the source of the defective blades and that the defect could no longer happen. He reached down the side of his desk and lifted up a beautiful brown leather case with my initials in gold on the corner, which he opened on his desk to reveal one of every product made by Gillette's including a gold plated Gillette razor all fitted into a red velvet lining and said: "Please except this token of our appreciation."

Talking to Woodgate afterwards I got the whole story. There had been a gang of six engineers who maintained production lines for razorblades, which were minded by women who had a one-hour lunch break at midday. The machines had to be run continuously, so one of the maintenance gang stood in for each woman going for lunch. The foreman of the maintenance gang saw a way of making some money. The gang made up a replacement die stamp deliberately offset, which they fitted to the machine directly the minder went to lunch.

The machines each produced some thousand blades an hour and at the end of the line just before packing there was an automatic quality control section. Any blade not up to standard was side tracked into a scrap container for recycling. Of course, the offset blades were side tracked where they were collected by the maintenance gang and fed back into the line after the counter but before the packing. The packs of twenty by five blades were collected by the maintenance men. The offset die was removed before the minder returned from lunch, and no one was any

Chapter 6

the wiser about what had been happening. The maintenance gang smuggled the packs of blades out of the factory in their cars and sold them to dodgy outlets like market traders. The foreman of the maintenance gang was sent to prison for I think nine months, his assistant got six months and the rest of the gang were sacked.

I did not have the heart to tell the Gillette people that I had taken to electric shaving and had no use for their magnificent gift. However I had my initials blanked out and the presentation case made a superb wedding present for a friend who got married shortly afterwards.

Before I was married I had become friends with Ted Wilkes and his wife Vera who lived opposite my parents in Comptons Lane. Ted had come over one Sunday morning to see the Austin 750 Formula car I was building in my parents' garage.

It transpired that I had met and became friends with the most talented person I ever knew.

Ted Wilkes had built and raced a famous speed hill climb special car, the Wilkes G.N. before World War II and had done very well with it. This car is recorded in the several books about pre-War Shelsey Walsh hill climb specials. Throughout the War Ted had worked as a designer in the British car industry rising to Chief Designer, for I think, the Routes Group. In this role he was invited to design and build 'The Car of the Future' for the Festival of Britain held in 1951. This he did, the car featuring in the Dome of Discovery.

Influences

I distinctly remember seeing the car at the festival. This car was regarded as a very far-out concept design of a type unlikely ever to be built. This car had no bonnet, the screen was at the front to give maximum internal space and there were three rows of seats for six people completely unlike any car then available. Some forty years later all the design features of Ted's car appeared in the acclaimed revolutionary Renault Espace, which spawned all the subsequent people carrier type of cars.

So Ted initiated a whole unique type of car.

Sometime after the Festival of Britain, Ted with a partner named Ashmore set up an industrial design practice based, for reasons I never knew, in Horsham. His office and workshop was in Blatchford Road and he lived, as mentioned, in Comptons Lane. We saw a good deal of each other in the intervening years, Ted became Godfather to my son Nick and I was continually amazed by his artistic skills. He was a very accomplished watercolour painter and a world-class designer. One project he had which stands out in my memory was when he was commissioned by the manufacturers of Frigidaire Refrigerators to design a new range. At that time all refrigerators had rounded corners and fluting decoration so that they resembled the jukeboxes of that period.

Ted designed a new style of refrigerator with clean lines and sharp corners, which became known as the Ice Diamond. Frigidaire were very

Chapter 6

excited by Ted's design and were anxious to show an example of this new style of fridge at the upcoming Ideal Home Exhibition then only a couple of months away. This was far too short a time to make all of the patterns and press-tools for production so they asked Ted if he could make a full sized model of the external shape and appearance of the mid range refrigerator which they could show at the Ideal Home Exhibition.

Ted took this on only if they agreed to him making a complete model refrigerator, which was to be the same as the production unit in all respects. Ted produced, weighted as appropriate, in wood a complete refrigerator with opening door, shelves and racks inside, etc which stood on the Frigidaire stand for two weeks of the show where thousands of people looked all round it, opened the doors, moved the shelves and generally inspected the refrigerator without realising it was a wooden mock-up. Pretty clever I think. This Ice Diamond refrigerator went onto the market not long after and for many years was the biggest selling benchmark refrigerator in Britain and the USA.

Ted Wilkes designed many, if not most of the domestic products, which became available in the ensuing years. Examples that come to mind are a range of door furniture, domestic electric kettles and electric irons. One big project was the design of the cab and external body work of the Deltic Diesel-Electric Railway Locomotive for British Rail

Influences

which included an ergonomic driver's seat which set the design criteria for industrial seating for all time.

The foreman in charge of Ted's workshop was John Woodhatch, a childhood friend of mine whose father and mother had run a little general shop in Highlands Road in Horsham a few yards from Highlands Avenue where I lived during the War. John came and worked with me in the evenings and weekends on various projects, mainly boat building, from the mid 1960s and he still acts as my Managing Agent for my offices in Foundry Lane.

I embarked on building a new special car based on a Fiat 500 chassis with a 1000cc BMC A type engine. This was in the very early days of the glass reinforced plastic (GRP) which I wanted to use to construct the body. Ted Wilkes undertook the design of this body and produced detailed drawings of a very beautiful body, nicer than any car designs then available including the exotic Italians.

I was to build this body in GRP on a male mould; that is, you created the desired shaped then cast the GRP on the outside and removed the mould from the inside after the body was cast. My mould was in plaster of Paris on a chicken wire matrix and I am ashamed to say that while the body bore some resemblance to that which Ted Wilkes designed my limited skill failed to produce

Chapter 6

the subtle shapes and features, so the result was not quite what Ted and I had hoped.

Ted and Vera Wilkes remained our friends until first Vera then Ted died in the 1980s in Petworth to where they had retired.

The death of a contemporary, Harold Hobbs, at a young age brought me up with a bit of a jerk. At that time, as now, we were continually bombarded with what we should and should not eat and drink. Although it is interesting to note that the instructions then were completely different to those now. The most outstanding example was the 'drink-a-pinta-milk-a-day' campaign which was widespread for years with posters featuring a girl with a white stripe in her dark hair pageboy bob, and the half pint of milk issued every day to every school child from the start of World War II. Now we are told that you should not drink much milk! And the school milk has long since been discontinued.

At the time I am referring to the major thrust of all this public health information was heart attacks from heart disease. I earnestly took all this information to 'heart' until one week when three people I knew all died of heart attacks within a few days of each other. The first of these on 30th November 1982 was my good friend Eric Thompson who has been mentioned elsewhere. Eric, a television presenter of a children's programme, only ate healthy food and I don't think he actually drank alcohol, certainly there

Influences

was nothing but water when I went to dinner and he did not smoke. The next was Bill Grant about the same age as me and the larger of the two Grant brothers whom I had known from childhood. Bill was about six foot four inches tall, weighed about eighteen stone, played rugby for Sussex and was a builder doing hard manual work. His party trick was to go up a ladder with a full one hundred weight cement bag under each arm. Bill was a non-smoker but did like a pint or two of beer in the evening.

The third on 16th December 1982 was Colin Chapman of Lotus car fame, an acquaintance from the 750 Motor Club. Colin Chapman at this time had come a long way from his first Lotus, an Austin 7 Special, to being the world leading designer and builder of Formula 1 Grand Prix cars and in partnership with DeLorean conning millions of pounds out of the British Government. Colin Chapman lived the high-life with private aircraft, parties every night, lots of time in Monte Carlo, the best restaurants and chain-smoking cigars.

All these three with completely different lifestyles and of about my age, died of heart attacks within a couple of weeks of each other. So I decided to take the health advice that we are subjected to at every turn with a pinch of salt and steer a moderate course.

Chapter 7 - Family and other matters

I got to know Jane Beney when she started to commute into London on the same trains as me, we both travelled in the Buffet Car on the way up in the morning as this was a social gathering of the same people each day. Jane was at that time resting after acting in repertory theatre at Burnham-on-Sea, Somerset and was working as a receptionist in Scholl's, Regent Sheet. Jane was very glamorous with a cache of being an actress and by far the most attractive girl travelling. So in spite of attentions by some others I managed to gain her interest and we began to see each other elsewhere than on the train.

I suspect at the instigation of her mother, I was summoned for inspection to a party her parents were holding in their biggish house in Warnham Road, Horsham. I went along and found that all the other guests were of my parent's generation with whom I had nothing in common. Jane was busy serving drinks and things so I was at a bit of a loose end. I took my half pint of bitter and went to sit out of the way in the big inglenook fireplace in the room adjoining the party. After I had been there some time I was joined by a man named Young, the long time manager of Barclays Bank in Horsham whom I knew as the father of a chap I played cricket against. Anyway, Young had drunk too much and was very garrulous. It transpired he was about to retire from the bank where he'd never liked working. Apparently many years before he had a customer with a market garden who went bankrupt. When the bank foreclosed Young had the chance to buy the market garden cheaply. It was a dream come true for him as he had always wanted a market garden. However the lure of a secure job and a pension kept him at the bank and he had regretted not taking the opportunity ever since, particularly now he was retiring and had nothing to look forward to. He said to me "Young man if you see an opportunity take it, or you will regret not having done so for the rest of your life".

Frankly I found Young's outpourings embarrassing, so I made my excuses to Jane's parents and left to walk the two or so miles home on the crisp and frosty night. Walking along I thought deeply of what Young had said and decided to take that advice on board. I have applied that advice throughout my life and passed it on to my children, all of whom have complied with great success. The point is that if you go for an opportunity when it presents itself and the project goes belly up after a year or so you can always go back to what you were doing previously.

This party and subsequent meetings enabled me to get to know Jane's parents whom I had only known by sight previously. Jane's father was a tall dapper mild mannered man who, like my father,

Chapter 7

worked for British Rail in the offices at Waterloo, and although they knew each other they had no social contact, I suspect that Jane's father was lower down the office hierarchy than my father. The main feature of Jane's father was that he was the archetype hen pecked husband. Jane's mother was a smallish belligerent woman who had to be in charge all the time. She was a real live wire who had an opinion on everything and gave it out whether it was wanted or not. She despised her husband and made no bones about showing it and had to be in control of everything she was involved in. This had a deep impact on Jane's upbringing. Being an only child Jane had been indulged by her mother and imbued with her mother's fearsome prejudices. As can be gathered I did not like Mrs Beney and I was not surprised that she did not seem to have any friends.

Anyway Jane and I saw more and more of each other, became engaged and finally married. It should be understood that in my day when you had been going out with somebody for some time you just slid into marriage without any conscious decision by either party because it was the done thing which was expected of you by all your friends and family. I think the modern system of living together as a trial marriage, which can be terminated without any recrimination and financial complications, to be a much better arrangement.

We had a full-blown wedding on the 23rd November 1957 in Horsham Parish Church and reception at Lynwood Country Club with all the bells and whistles. We left for our honeymoon, in my Fiat 500 with poor battery, so Jane in all her finery had to push start it.

We were very lucky to rent Manor Cottage a little further up Comptons Lane from where my parents lived. This small house was owned by an old lady living in Littlehampton and was not in very good order having been let out for many years. As all houses of the period it had single glazed Crittall metal windows, suspended floors, no insulation anywhere and no central heating. As a result it was a desperately cold house in which we lived for some ten years and where we had our three children. When we first got married we literally had no money. We could not afford to furnish Manor Cottage and existed for some time eating off a borrowed folding card table and sitting on boxes, while I designed and built furniture from steel rods welded up in my parents garage. This is not as bad as it now sounds as this steel rod Scandinavian style furniture was all the rage at the time.

Over the period of a couple of years I did manage to furnish the whole house other than the dining room at the back of the ground floor which was my workshop.

Chapter 7

The pinnacle of my furniture building was a double bed known in the family as 'The Great Iron'.

Jane has always been a noisy and restless sleeper and a normal double bed in which the occupants end up together in the middle meant I got very little sleep. So I designed our bed with two separate hammock like compartments, each sprung with rubber strips and with a separating sub-structure. The whole bed was constructed on engineering principals as a space frame from one inch square tube and was so rigid that restless movements by one occupant were undetectable to the other. With a double foam mattress this bed gave us comfortable nights for many years and eventually, regrettably, was cut up when we moved to Merston Cottage and found that we could not get 'The Great Iron' up the very small staircase and landing.

Bearing in mind that I was working in London at G N Hadens leaving home at 07:15 in the morning and getting back at 19:30 at the earliest in the evening for five days a week then doing things inside the house, this did not give any time to do anything in the considerable size garden which in consequence became overgrown and derelict, particularly the back garden. This gave rise to complaints from the neighbours. I constantly intended to get in a contractor to sort out the garden but could never afford it.

Family and other matters

On the 24th September 1958 our son Nicholas Stuart was born in the maternity unit of Horsham Hospital in Hurst Road. It was a straightforward birth and Jane stayed in hospital for the standard ten days usual at that time.

As a surprise for her return from hospital I decided to decorate our main room at the front of the house in colours that we had discussed and agreed and which included one wall brick red. I was not getting home until about 9pm after catching the return train to Horsham, followed by a one mile mile walk from the station to visit Jane in hospital and then a two mile walk home. After something to eat this gave me a maximum of about two hours before I had to go to bed to get up at 06:00 next morning.

Things went quite well until I painted the brick red wall. It was a disaster, it made the room dark and oppressive. Not being around to shop for paint, I fortunately found some yellow paint we had left over from decorating the kitchen. I had to use several coats of this yellow to mask the brick red and this put the planned programme back so that I had to work right through the Friday night for Jane and Nick's homecoming on Saturday. When Jane came home her only comment was that it was a pity that the wall was not brick red.

Nick was a good baby and caused us little trouble except once when his high chair shut up and pitched him down on the front doorstep onto

Chapter 7

his face which gave him a fat upper lip with a slightly upturned nose which are with him for life.

When Nick was young our regular friends were Betty Spratt, Horsham's most glamorous blonde who worked in Trevor Cale, the chemist, and whom I'd known from my school days and her then permanent boyfriend, Keith Gray who lived in Cowfold. Keith Gray was about four years older than me, after a 'good' War he was then a racing car mechanic. Keith and I had an immediate affinity and became the good friends we remain to this day. Just as an aside, after being engaged for fourteen years, Bet and Keith eventually got married.

Our other close friends were a Canadian couple spending a year working in England as a honeymoon; they were Dave and Sandra Scarth. Through me Dave Scarth bought an enormous Audi touring car which we thought was a German staff car booty from the War. This was a big car which we all, including Nick, spent many hours and covered many miles going all round the South of England so that the Scarths could do the tourist thing. They were good and carefree days which ended when the Scarths went back to Canada. Before this Dave and I had spent many hours planning what we each thought would be our dream house. Dave's to be built in Canada and entirely different to mine to be built in the UK. Canadian thinking was for Dave to build his house in wood, not then permissible under British building regulations. Being an engineer I could see no point in building a house from imitation stone blocks (bricks) stuck together with a very rigid but poor adhesive (mortar) and hence my house was steel framed with infill panels which were not masonry.

After the departure of the Scarths to Canada, Jane's and my life continued as before and in due time Lisa Jane was born on the 13th November 1962 followed by Rachel Clare on the 3rd September 1964. All the children were fine and healthy and we grew up as a reasonably happy family making the best of the increasingly unsatisfactory Manor Cottage. We never seemed to have enough money, certainly we could never save any significant amount.

We have kept in touch with the Scarths ever since. Dave became a successful Architect and Sandra rose in the Canadian Civil Service. We had a memorable three week holiday with them in Canada and they have visited England for a week or ten day visits some four or five times over the years and stayed with us. One reason why they came to England so comparatively frequently was because Dave is one of a pair of twins, he and his brother had for years been writing a history of their family and had pieced together the complete story back to the Middle Ages when the Scarth family were deeply involved in the town of Scarborough. Dave claimed that in medieval times

Chapter 7

the town was called Scarthborough and was owned by his family.

However, there was one piece of history they had been unable to obtain. This concerned an uncle who had died during WW2 – but the circumstances were known only to Dave's grandmother who, for some reason, would not say what happened. This uncle named Bill Coulson had been a gung-ho bush pilot in the early thirties who had graduated to fly Lockheed 14 Super Electrons for Trans Canadian Airlines. The military version of this aircraft was the Lockheed 14 Hudson supplied to the RAF for WW2. In 1939 Bill Coulson joined the RAF and because of his wide pre-war experience with the civilian Lockheed 14 he was appointed as expert and instructor on Hudsons at RAF Silloth in Scotland with the rank of Squadron Leader.

To be frank, everyone found Dave's obsession with this family history was a bit of a bore, so during this particular visit I tried to put him off getting me to drive him around on what I thought was a wild goose chase. Anyway, Dave kept badgering me to take him to "Southleigh" Aerodrome which he had heard was connected with his uncle's death. I pointed out that there was no such place as "Southleigh" aerodrome, but he might mean Eastleigh Airport, the airport for Southampton. So after lunch on a miserable wet Thursday afternoon I drove Dave to Eastleigh Airport, advising him that this was now a small commercial airport, unlikely to have any information about the war years.

So it proved, all the people in the departure area were twenty years old and knew nothing about the War. However, they suggested we went to a museum housed in one of the wartime hangers. This museum turned out to be a general museum which had been associated with a restaurant in Warnham, near Horsham, which had been closed down by the Public Health people when half of a German Shepherd dog had been found in their larder. The museum had been moved to Eastleigh Airport.

Entrance to the museum was through a fully lit hut in which there was a young man selling books and souvenirs of the wartime RAF at Eastleigh while the museum itself was in darkness as there were no visitors. This young chap knew nothing about Dave's uncle and Dave continuing to cross question him I found embarrassing, so I went out on my own to look round what of the museum I could see in the gloom. I had not been out for long when Dave came to the doorway of the book hut and called for me to come back. When I did so I found that he had been joined by a late middle-aged couple. "Listen to what this chap has to tell us," said Dave.

It turned out that this chap had been an RAF Apprentice at Eastleigh during the War. After the War he had returned to the north of England and had not been South until he had some holiday

Chapter 7

owing and had come with his wife to tour for a few days. This day they had passed Eastleigh by chance and the husband had said that he had been there during the War and they should have a look round. They had come into the museum and heard Dave trying to get information about his uncle. The chap had interrupted Dave by saying that he had been there and as a witness knew all about it.

This chap gave us broadly the following account which we have been able to verify and augment from various sources.

There was a requirement to deliver two of the Hudson planes at Silloth to be refitted with photo reconnaissance equipment by Cunliffe Owen, the experts in this field, whose works and hangars were on RAF Eastleigh airfield near Southampton. So on 15th August 1940 a flight comprising the two Hudsons to be refitted led by a third Hudson piloted by Bill Coulson to bring the delivery crews back to Silloth that evening set off from Scotland. Each Hudson contained a pilot, co-pilot and a gunner, while Bill Coulson's plane had an additional civilian passenger, a Jack Whittaker who worked for Sperry, the gyroscope manufacturers and who had an urgent need to get to Northolt Aerodrome, north of London, and Bill Coulson had agreed to drop him off there on the way back to Scotland.

At this time the Southampton area was under regular attack by German bombers aiming to destroy the factory building Spitfires. When air attacks were expected barrage balloons, tethered by wire cables were flown round Southampton and Eastleigh airfield to prevent low level attacks. So that the RAF could use Eastleigh unless an attack was actually in progress the ring of barrage balloons had an opening at the North and South ends at each of which a lorry mounted quick deployable barrage balloon was kept down, only to be put up when the attack occurred.

Approaching the area of Southampton Bill Coulson's flight spotted a large number of German bombers with a raid in progress so he landed his flight at Nether Wallop until the raid had cleared the area, whereupon he proceeded to Eastleigh.

The following is the account given by the chap who had been an eyewitness.

Bill Coulson prepared for the return flight with, in addition to his own crew, the three crew of each of the other two Hudsons and Jack Whittaker on board. During actual take-off the air raid warning siren sounded which prompted the release of the barrage balloons at the North and South gates.

Bill Coulson flying out of the North gate flew into the balloon cable and crashed onto a house adjoining the airfield, number 195 Nutbourne Road, Eastleigh, killing all twelve people in the aircraft and Mr and Mrs Craig who lived in the house. The chap who had been at Eastleigh at the time even pointed out the house concerned which, of course had long since been rebuilt.

Chapter 7

"Right," said Dave to me. "Let's go round to that house." So I drove out of the airport and round to the house in a road of pairs of semi detached houses. I parked outside and Dave knocked on the door for some time but there was no answer. Obviously the occupants were out. We went to the car and were wondering what to do next when a young woman with a child in a pushchair accompanied by an elderly woman came down the pavement and turned into the house next door. Dave rushed up to them and asked if they knew anything about the plane crash in the War which had killed his uncle. The elderly woman immediately attacked Dave. As a young woman she had been living in an adjoining house when the plane crashed. Although uninjured the experience had been so traumatic that it deeply affected her. For forty years she had been looking for someone to blame. Now Dave was that person. Dave was so taken aback by this attack that he fled back to the car and we drove away.

Dave said "Let's go into Southampton to the local newpaper office and see if we can find out any more about the crash." It was about five in the afternoon by this time and I said to Dave that it was unlikely that the newspaper office would be open. However, he insisted and when we found the newspaper office it was on the point of closing. Dave did the Canadian visitor tactic and persuaded the one employee left in the office to let him look through the archive copies of papers at the time of the accident. These records were on microfiche and after scrolling through quite a number we found a very small paragraph about the crash. The substance of which was to blame the pilot Bill Coulson for killing the five young pilots, three aircrew, two civilians and a boffin, along with himself, at a time when Britain needed every pilot it could get.

This newspaper piece itself – or something very similar – must have been received by Dave's grandmother. She had Bill Coulson's body brought back to Canada for burial in a secret ceremony and kept the circumstances of his death secret because she was so ashamed.

Dave was satisfied that he now had the complete and true story of his uncle's death, although subsequently Jane and I did some further research and tracked down the graves of the passengers in the plane in a cemetery in Hamble.

Dave and his relations have just issued their book The Airman, Bill Coulson, giving a full account of his life and death! I have a copy of that book.

What impressed me was the extraordinary coincidence of the man who had been an RAF Apprentice coming to Eastleigh and the museum some forty years later exactly when Dave Scarth happened to be there. However, this is not the end of the coincidence in this visit by Dave Scarth.

Chapter 7

Dave and Sandra were flying back to Canada on the Saturday following the Thursday we had gone to Eastleigh. The Scarths, Jane and I went out to dinner on the Friday evening to a little restaurant we used occasionally which was located at the top of Denne Road in Horsham which was run by a young couple, the husband was Italian and did the cooking and his English wife ran the restaurant.

When it came to choosing pudding, Dave wanted ice cream of which there were a selection on the Menu. Dave asked the wife for an explanation of one ice cream variety listed as a CA Special. The wife explained that she had the recipe for this ice cream from her Aunt Cecily Anne who she had recently visited in Canada.

Dave said: "Does your aunt live in Toronto?"

"Yes," said the girl.

"And is her name Tomkins?"

"Yes" said the girl.

Dave replied that he and Sandra were great friends with Aunt Cecily Anne who lived two streets away from their house and they had her to dinner two weeks previously. Another extraordinary coincidence.

It eventually dawned on me that the only way we were going to move from rented Manor Cottage was if I actually built my own dream house myself. After being unable to find a suitable building plot through Horsham estate agents I put a wanted small ad in the Horsham local paper,

The West Sussex County Times, which to my astonishment produced eleven replies. In the end only one was practical from a price and planning permission perspective. This was one of the plots in Forest Road, Horsham sold off in the 1930s by Gillette, a farmer whose son David was contemporary with me at Collyers School. Years later after his father had died the residue of the original farm was bought for the South Holmes Housing Association where I was a Consulting Engineer for the District Heating Scheme.

The deceased husband of the elderly lady offering me half of her garden had bought two plots originally, had a house build on one and used the other plot as an extended garden. In consequence the piece of land was only forty feet wide but three hundred feet deep, front to back. I thought I could make something of that plot and bought it for £1500 which was a fair price for those days.

I developed my steel frame house design for this narrow plot and with some presentation help from John Warren, a school friend who had qualified as an architect, I submitted planning and building bye-laws applications to Horsham Rural Council.

The results were two surprises. The design of the house was far-out modern by the standards of those days completely different from all the other houses in Forest Road which were 1930s style, yet unconditional planning permission was granted.

Chapter 7

However the building bye-laws application was categorically refused on the basis that the vertical steel stanchions and supports had to be encased in at least four and half inches of brickwork. The reason put forward was that in the event of fire the steel would soften and allow the building to collapse whereas the brickwork would not. My argument that there was widespread use of steel framed industrial buildings without vertical encasement did not persuade the Council, so I removed the vertical steels and replaced them with brick piers and columns to satisfy the bye-laws. I never pointed out that all the horizontal structures supporting the floors and roof were steel and these were never queried.

The design was for a two storey front section with a single storey rear extension and a double garage detached at right angles across the front. This provided ground floor accommodation, sitting room, dining room, kitchen, utility, playroom, study and small workshop. While upstairs there were two large bedrooms, two small bedrooms and a bathroom. All rooms light and airy. The design contained no wasted space and to this principle I decided on mono-pitched roofs without the waste of a loft space.

I set to build this house myself with latterly some amateur part-time help from Dennis and John Reeves, sons of Reeves The Butchers in Roffey, and Alan Knight, unkindly referred to as the Roffey Village Idiot, as labourer. With intermittent help from this motley gang I spent every moment that I was not at work or asleep for three and a half years building my dream house into a very nice, much admired and then very modern family house. On completion this house was written up in The Architects Journal.

The land behind my plot fell to a stream edging St Leonards Forest, the valley being named on the Ordinance Survey map as Severals Bottom. I called my completed house Severals House which I thought appropriate for the various miscellaneous friends that had helped me build it. The design was successful except in one minor aspect. The roofs, which had a pitch too shallow for tiles or slates, were clad in an aluminium profile called Snaprib. This was fine except that when it rained the roof drummed and on sunny days with little clouds the roof would expand and contract with loud clicking noises as the sun was alternatively exposed and obscured.

The Cuban Missile Crisis when Russia and America were on the verge of nuclear war occurred during the early stages of building this house. Foreman & Partners, whose Brighton office I was then running, were issued with Government design criteria features for nuclear fallout shelters to be built for Government buildings. Using that data I designed and built an underground shelter beneath the garage. The threat of nuclear war diminished but the shelter remained – I suspect the only private nuclear fallout shelter built at

Chapter 7

that time. The fallout shelter should have enhanced the value of the house enormously but for the fact that I could not advertise its existence for obvious reasons. This shelter remains to this day after certainly three changes of house ownership.

Photo 3: Severals House from the back

Jane and I and our three children moved into Severals House and enjoyed our life there. The children went to Colgate County Primary School an old style village school about three miles up the road from our house. We found Colgate School to be excellent and far removed from the urban schools in Horsham which were undergoing Government directed education improvements such as 'new maths', which the lapse of time has proved to be unsatisfactory.

Nick grew out of Colgate School and as the only nearby source of friends was Roffey, which was the down market end of Horsham I invoked the old boy net with the County Council people that I knew through business and managed to get Nick into Steyning Grammar School as a boarder. Steyning Grammar School had a very good reputation and I was very pleased to get this place which I thought would give Nick a very good educational opportunity.

After we had lived in Severals House for some ten years I had to make the commercial decision to buy Westlands in Kings Road Horsham, as described elsewhere. I very reluctantly sold Severals House, my own design and build dream house for £25,000 which showed me a profit of some £20,000 so all my effort had produced a dividend. Out of interest Severals House unaltered sold in the 1990s for £450,000.

Westlands, Kings Road Horsham was designed and built by an architect in 1900 for his own use.

It was a very well build spacious five bedroom house with some unusual features, which included a two storey leaded light window to a magnificent oak staircase from the hall to a galleried landing. The interior had remained untouched since it was built in the Victorian style and was thus very dark and gloomy with dark stained interior woodwork and a big hall with hideous dark glazed tiles on all the walls up to about four feet. I set to and brightened the place

Chapter 7

up by redecorating throughout, painting the doors and all the internal woodwork white and covering the Hall tiles with oak panelling. When I bought Westlands it only had a virtually derelict detached timber garage probably added in the 1930s as originally the 'motor house' had been part of Westlands cottage, then my offices in Foundry Lane. I designed and built a three-car garage with a one bedroom flat over, built in conventional brick to match the house and an external spiral concrete staircase. The flat was an afterthought and was for Jane's mother. Jane's father had died a few months before the garage project had started and it gave an ideal opportunity for Jane's mother to move back to Horsham from Bracknell where she was then living. When she moved into this flat Jane's mother was showing the beginnings of dementia which affliction gradually worsened over the three or four years before she died of a bronchial failure.

While living in Westlands first Lisa then Rachel outgrew Colgate School. Jane was adamant that the girls should not go to a State school and so we sent them to a very expensive private school, Farlington at Broadbridge Heath near Horsham. This proved to be a mistake. Farlington essentially catered for girls who were either backward or who had been dumped there by their rich parents who were off abroad being diplomats or similar. The result was that our girls' peers were either spoilt rotten or were psychologically disturbed. Not an ideal environment to spend your school days. It took several years for me to get Jane to accept the obvious shortcomings of this school. She eventually agreed to send both girls to the local comprehensive but unfortunately it was too late, particularly in the case of Lisa who joined only a year or so before O levels with less academic knowledge than even the most delinquent and stupid of the pupils at the comprehensive school. Ultimately Lisa declined to even sit her O levels and thus left school with no academic qualifications whatsoever. Rachel fared a little better having an additional year or so to get on track.

In retrospect snobbery ruined the education of both girls although it must be said that after this bad start they have both been very successful in their various ways.

Nick's education was not much better than that of his sisters. While his term reports from Steyning Grammar School showed average progress, when he ultimately took his O levels he passed one only. I could not let his education stop at one O level and as he had already left Steyning I decided he should live at home and study for more O levels the following year. The only school with the same syllabus as Steyning was Holy Trinity in Crawley – so that is where he went. I had great difficulty in getting him to study but in the end he got three further O levels to make a total of four. With which his schooling finished.

Chapter 7

I then tried to find a career for Nick. We got books from the library which listed every career imaginable but to start most you needed better O levels results than Nick achieved, while none of the others was he prepared to even consider. So we reached stalemate. I would not let him sit about the house all day while his mother and I were at work so I insisted he got a job until he decided on a career. Nick was very good about this and got a series of shop assistant jobs with Millets (outdoor clothing), Scott and Sargent (ironmongers) and finally Vinds (men's flash suit tailor). The last job he was really interested in so his world reduced to suiting cloth, width of lapels and diameter of bottom of trouser legs. A very limited outlook on life. I deplored the absence of the National Service I had done, which took young men away from cosseted home life and set them square into the adult world. This worried me and I discussed my concerns with Geoffrey Pearce, my friend and solicitor. Geoff suggested I create a similar effect to National Service by getting Nick to go and work abroad for a year or so. It must be understood that this was long before the current common practice of young people taking a "gap year" to travel the world. I thought this was a grand idea and after discussing it with Jane we agreed to put our offer to him on his eighteenth birthday due in about six weeks.

The family practice for birthdays was to give cards and presents at breakfast. This is what Lisa and Rachel did. I did not but said to Nick would he please come home from work rather than go straight out for the evening. This was normally a sign that he was in trouble over something. Anyway, he duly came home in the evening and Jane and I sat him in our sitting room and told him "For your eighteenth birthday we will buy your ticket to anywhere in the world that you want to go and we will pay you £50 per month for one year. The money is not to live on but to create an emergency fund so that if you get stuck somewhere and need to move on, at least you will have some money to get to the next stop on the bus."

I thought a great deal about how excited I would have been to get an offer like that for my eighteenth birthday. Nick's reaction completely stunned me. He went chalk white and asked if he could go to bed. This was about 6.30 in the evening. After he had gone up Jane and I discussed his reaction and agreed he had probably not understood our proposal. The next day I ran over it again with a similar reaction. Thereafter Nick's life carried on as before – he made no mention of the World Trip.

We used to take the Sunday Times newspaper which had pages of jobs, a lot of them abroad. I found one, a six-month contract for drivers of gigantic dumper trucks for an open cast mine near Alice Springs in Australia. The pay was fantastic, for six months you lived, all found, in a

Chapter 7

site hotel and received pocket money. At the end of six months you were paid £25,000 sterling, which in the mid 1970s was a great deal of money.

Nick refused to even consider this job. I felt I couldn't just leave the trip offer to drift on indefinitely so I found another advertisement in a later Sunday Times, this time looking for recruits for Kibbutz in Israel. I filled up the form and got Nick to sign it and sent it off. Nick was accepted and given a flight out by El Al on a date about four weeks later. Nick did not react at all when I handed him the booking. As the departure time approached it was obvious from his demeanor that he was going to refuse to go to Israel. This put me in a difficult position. I could not physically force an eighteen-year- old man to go, so I did not know what to do. Then I had a real stroke of luck.

Nick met a Steyning Grammar School chum in The Bear Pub in Horsham which adjoined the offices of The West Sussex County Times, our local newspaper. The chum had just joined the paper as a cub reporter and was looking for his first story. Nick told him that he was being banished from his family by his evil father and sent as slave labour to Israel. Of course, this reporter latched on to this story and obtained permission from his Editor to write a full-page piece on it. Unknown to me this reporter with a cameraman came to our house and took a posed picture of Nick sitting between his sisters, specially dressed for the occasion, all looking at a map of Israel in an Atlas. This picture and a full-page article appeared in that week's West Sussex County Times. The article was not very complimentary to me. The result of this article was not what I think Nick expected. He received lots of sympathy for his evil father and became a local hero.

This celebrity status forced Nick to go through with the Israel trip, so, we took him to London Airport on the appointed day and saw off a rather sad figure. On the way home I worried whether I had done the right thing. Nick had promised to write every day, but in the event we heard nothing from him for about a month. We were by then very worried and about to get on to the Israeli embassy for an investigation when a parcel the size of a house brick was delivered. This was indeed Nick's letters, written every day but posted as one lot a month later. The post revealed that Nick thought we were all fools living in England. The life in the Kibbutz was the only way to be and he was never coming home. Obviously he had settled in and the whole thing was working well.

In fact Nick stayed in Israel for about ten months and came back with Anna, a Danish girlfriend, in tow. She was not a very nice girl in many ways. Nick got a job locally to earn some money while Anna stayed in bed all morning, until Jane and I came home for lunch. Anna would not

Chapter 7

help to get lunch or wash up afterwards. She spent the afternoon bathing and washing her hair and watching television until Nick came home when she demanded to be taken out for the evening. I couldn't let this go on so I suggested to Nick that she got a job and found somewhere else to live. This upset him so he decided they would both leave and go and live with Jane's mother in Bracknell. I knew this was going to be a disaster.

Anna lasted a week in Bracknell and then went back to Denmark never to be heard from again. Jane's mother bullied Nick into getting a job as a negotiator with a Bracknell Estate Agent. This was a master stroke as Nick adopted estate agency as a career and became very successful. So my creation of a version of National Service worked out just fine in Nick's case.

Chapter 8 - Dogs

When I was about nine years old after much pleading my parents bought me an accidental cross breed puppy from a kennels at Faygate near Horsham. This dog had some Irish terrier blood so he was named Paddy and grew into a super medium size dog that I loved deeply. Paddy used to come with me everywhere, riding in a basket on my bike for long journeys. I had a friend of about my own age named Peter Matthews who lived near me in Highlands Crescent and had a bitch called Poppy, very similar in size and coat to Paddy. These two dogs fell in love and were constant companions when they were able. They never produced any puppies, I don't know why, certainly not due to us keeping them apart.

So I spent my teenage years inseparable from my dog Paddy, roaming St Leonards forest, fishing in lakes around Horsham and doing the things that boys did in those days. Growing up close together with Paddy we understood how each others minds worked and I never remember having to shout at or smack Paddy for doing something wrong, we just acted as a team. This experience gave me what I hope is a not misplaced ability to understand dogs. That is dogs with enough brain to think properly. Some toy and small dogs I am not so good with. Anyway the

Chapter 8

absence of dominating commands between myself and Paddy was his downfall.

I came home on my first Christmas leave during National Service and Paddy, who had obviously missed me, was very excited. To calm him down I took him out for a short walk. Because of our relationship I never had Paddy on a lead, it was not normally necessary. But on this fateful occasion just after leaving the house in Cambridge Road, Horsham we came to Clarence Road, a busy through road where hyper excited Paddy saw a cat on the opposite side of the road and before I realised what was happening he darted across the road straight under the wheels of a passing car. He died in my arms at the kerbside. I was mortified and swore never to risk such an upset again by never having another dog. I stuck to that decision for many years.

While living in Severals House we embarked on family dogs. The children wanted a dog so I bought 'The Observers Book of Dogs' which we all studied and decided on a Wire Haired Dachshund, we acquired a puppy and named him Benny. He turned out to be a great characterful little dog.

We thought he might be lonely when we were out so we bought successively Bracken, a black and silver Wire Haired Dachshund and then Helga who was a standard Wire Haired Dachshund. This family of dogs gave us great pleasure while the children were growing up. The choice of breed was a good one as with little short legs Dachshunds do not require a great deal of walking, although each Sunday I used to take the dogs for a long walk in the fir tree plantation a little further up Forest Road.

Benny was the most characterful of these dogs. At a Colgate School jumble sale for a bit of fun we bought for Benny a very young baby's tee-shirt, green with coloured stars. It fitted Benny perfectly and he then adopted this to wear all the time. I did not think it healthy for him to wear his tee-shirt at night and he got so angry that his eyes glowed red when we took it off him at bedtime to put in the wash. Dressed in his tee-shirt Benny would spend most of the day lying on his back with his legs in the air in a dolls pram which Lisa and Rachel would wheel round the garden, having pretend picnics, etc.

Eventually Benny was poisoned by a weird Spanish family who lived next door. He was replaced by another Wire Haired Dachshund by the name of Linus, so we had Bracken, Helga and Linus when we left Severals House and moved down to Westlands.

While living there we had another example of incorrect standard information about dogs' intelligence and mental ability. One Christmas the children bought a whoopee cushion which they put on my chair in the sitting room at Westlands. The children and dogs were in the room when I came in and sat on the whoopee cushion which

Chapter 8

performed as intended. Helga was absolutely captivated by this and without any question she laughed. We all spotted it and regularly throughout the day we set the cushion off with the same result. Helga laughed at whoopee cushions.

The dogs lived long and happy lives at Westlands but inevitably first Helga, then Bracken died peacefully of old age this left the much younger Linus.

At this time daughter Lisa who had then been married for some time had two dogs of her own, a German Shepherd and a Wire Haired Jack Russell and to prevent it being put down she took on a one year old all black German Shepherd bitch called Bella who had been returned to her breeder, a friend of Lisa's. Just before going for a month's sailing trip to the Mediterranean I met this dog and thought it a listless dull animal with not much going for it. When I came back from this sailing trip I found Bella living with us because she was unhappy being bullied by Lisa's dogs and Jane had taken pity and given her a home.

Although not best pleased I settled down to get to know Bella. The effect was quite extraordinary. When she came to us although her coat was black it was dull and grayish in colour which made her look dusty. Her head was always hanging down and her tail drooped between her legs. An unhappy dog. She took to me immediately and I spent a lot of time with her in the first few days.

Within a few weeks we had a transformed dog. Her coat was shiny black, her head was up and eyes bright and her tail was up and wagging most of the time.

She was a man's dog, and latched on to me to become my dog. She grew into a big powerful dog who spent all day with me in my office in Foundry Lane at the bottom of the garden. As we grew to know each other I began to realise the extent of the intelligence of German Shepherd dogs. They are far more intelligent than any other breed – bar none. Because of this they can be trained to do anything, guard dog, attack dog, guide dog or just loyal and protective family member. Wonderful animals, being largely free from breeders distortions and close physically to their wolf origins they are beautiful to look at as well.

When Bella was about five years old we thought she should have some pups. We searched everywhere for a pedigree all black male dog, eventually finding one at a breeder just outside Selsey. At the second attempt the mating was successful and Bella became pregnant. I read the books about dog births all of which said leave the dog alone as your presence may cause her to eat her newborn puppies. I built a birthing box which had a shelf around the inside under which the puppies could be protected from being laid on by their mother.

Late one evening, just before bedtime, Bella showed unmistakable signs that she was about to

Chapter 8

give birth so we settled her in her birthing box and intended to leave her alone. She cried and whined when we tried to leave, she wanted us to stay. Jane and I took half the night each. As each pup was born Bella pushed it over to us with her nose and left us to towel the puppy off, clearing the birth membrane and ensuring the puppy breathed, after which we put them into a separate box beside their mother.

By about 7am the following morning Bella had produced eight puppies and was so tired that she could not push anymore although she knew that not all her puppies had been born. We phoned the vet, whom we knew well, and he arrived to give Bella some stimulant which enabled her to produce two more puppies, which was the lot. We had ten German Shepherd puppies. The first born was a boy and significantly bigger than the others, we called him Bruno. The vet said of the last born and smallest that she was the runt of the litter and that she would not survive. We called her Purdy and successfully proved him wrong.

We decided to keep the first-born, Bruno, and the last-born, Purdy, but reluctantly decided that the others would have to find new homes. Fortunately it was summer time but the work and effort to raise ten puppies to the age of three months was immense, even though it was enormous fun. We let it be known that we had these puppies, I interviewed any applicants and if I thought them suitable would get them to sign a legal Agreement setting out the terms under which I would allow them to have a puppy and which also had a clause requiring them to return the dog to me in the event of them being unable to keep it for any reason.

We found a good home for all eight except for one where the applicants had lied and the dog was returned to us. His name was Rajah. So we ended up with mother Bella, daughter Purdy, sons Bruno and Rajah. All the local know-it-alls said you cannot keep two male dogs: they will fight for supremacy; you cannot keep two bitches they will quarrel and be constantly pursued by the male dogs. That turned out to be utter rubbish, Bella the mother was in charge and her children did as she told them. We never had any trouble with any of them throughout their long lives. They lived as a family without any interference from us.

When Bella gave birth we had little Linus, the last miniature Wire Haired Dachshund. Bella allowed him to be with her puppies almost from birth. Linus, who had always been in love with Bella, was convinced that he was the father of these puppies and was very proud of them. However as they grew much bigger than him he could be seen gazing at them in puzzlement at "how the hell did my puppies get so big." This family of dogs augmented by a mongrel called Spike who had been acquired by daughter Rachel but who lived with us, accompanied Jane and I

Chapter 8

when we retired to West Wittering. Here they lived happy lives walking on the beach and doing dog things in our one acre paddock.

As the years went by one by one the dogs died, Spike of a heart attack, Bella of old age, Bruno from the result of an unnecessary operation botched by a vet, then Rajah of old age and finally Purdy, the runt, the vet said we could not save, outlived them all and died at fourteen.

While Rajah and Purdy were still alive we obtained a pedigree black and tan bitch German Shepherd puppy from a local farm and called her Hannah. Hannah turned out to be the best dog we ever had. A sweet natured loving dog with extraordinary intelligence who never gave us any trouble and who had to be put down eventually at twelve due to chronic arthritis in her hips.

When Purdy died and Hannah was on her own we felt she needed a chum and Jane satisfied a life long ambition to own an Irish Wolfhound. This enormous bitch was one year old and named by her breeder, Peggy Sue. She was a sweet natured dog but not very bright in the mental department, however she fitted in very well with Hannah and lived to about eight years old, a very good age for an Irish Wolfhound.

Hannah was then on her own again and a friend asked us if we would take on a German Shepherd boy dog whose owners had to leave him alone all day while they were out at work. So we went over to Rose Green, Bognor to see this dog and hear his story. He is a standard black and tan dog his name is Frank and we think he was about five years old when he came to us.

He had a very unfortunate start in life. For his first six or nine months he was a feral stray dog living out of dustbins in Brighton. The RSPCA picked him up got him healthy, neutered him and homed him with a man in Brighton who loved him and looked after him well, but after a year or so became allergic to his fur. He went back to the RSPCA who then found him a home with the people we got him from, a one man band builder and his lady partner who only worked part-time. After a couple of years the builder had an accident at work which curtailed his building activities so that his income reduced and his partner had to go out to work full-time, leaving Frank at home alone all day which he does not like. So they were looking for someone to take Frank on.

I thought he was a super dog and though expecting all sorts of psychological problems from his early life we took Frank on. He has turned out to be a sweet natured loving companion with no faults at all except perhaps being a television addict, barking at animals on the screen.

Particularly the German Shepherd dogs have taught me many things – foremost of which is that anyone who does not like dogs is no good and not to be trusted. In spite of pretend shows of affection which a dog can see through, a dog will not respond to such a person and keeps clear but

Chapter 8

will keep watchful. This situation will go on for years even with someone they see frequently but eventually events will prove the dog's opinion of that person to be correct.

So that's my life with dogs. I am very grateful that I have been able to have dogs in appropriate conditions with enough space for them. My life would have been much poorer had I not had dogs.

Chapter 9 - Boats

My interest in boats was kindled at six or seven years old when I used to watch rowers in sliding seat skiffs on Highams Park lake. I remember it was the elegant shape of the Victorian style wooden single seat skiffs that fascinated and charmed me.

Later, boats featured in my frequent visits during WW2 to my cousins David and Dick in Clacton, Essex, a seaside town. Because there was a War on there was very little adult supervision, a great time to be a boy and to have all sorts of adventures without censure. We cycled all over the Clacton area and discovered St Osyth tide mill about three miles away which was isolated, unused and comprised a water mill fed by a tidal lake. The way the mill worked was for the lake to be filled by the rising tide, the gates closed at high water and as the outside water level fell on the ebb tide the lake water was released through the sluices to drive a mill wheel. Such tide mills were common around the coast in Victorian times. Of course they were very inefficient working at best for only six hours each day and for this reason the lake was very large to provide a lot of low-pressure water to work the wheel.

Chapter 9

The St Osyth mill lake was roughly circular and about half a mile in diameter with a small island in the middle. The water entry gates and channel to the wheel were sealed shut which retained the water at high level in the lake to be topped up only at high spring tides when the outside water level just topped the gates. To add to this wonderful place for boys, we found a boathouse at the edge of the lake with a twelve-foot clinker built wooden dinghy, gunter rigged and complete with an old sail, the boat was tied up with an easily undone rope painter. Of course we had to get the boat out onto the lake, hoist a sail and teach ourselves how to sail. This we did easily.

Just like Arthur Ransome's characters (whom we'd not heard of at that time) we sailed the boat virtually every day during the summer holidays and even camped over night on the island a couple of times. All of this without once seeing an adult or even other boys. After a couple of years' fun at St Osyth's the dinghy sank in the boathouse during a winter. We were unable to raise the boat and our time at St Osyth ended.

However our cycling out to St Osyth on a regular basis opened up another boating opportunity. On the way to St Osyth there were a number of big land-locked shallow lagoons containing brackish water. At this late stage of the War the RAF were flying some aircraft which needed their fuel tankage increased to reach far into the Continent of Europe. They achieved this by fitting drop tanks under each wing which had to be jettisoned before leaving the English coast and recovered for reuse. I cannot now recall which type of planes used these tanks but I believe one of them was the Mosquito.

The only way these tanks could be dropped without significant damage was into water. A couple of the lagoons near St.Osyth were selected for this exercise and we used to cycle past and see twenty or thirty of these drop tanks floating around and sometimes RAF personnel in waders collecting them up and loading the undamaged and reusable ones into lorries for recycling. The damaged ones they left either on the bank or just floating around. These tanks were of two types, one was a steel teardrop shape about eleven foot long, this steel type features in my later anecdote about Richard Reed's car.

The other type of tank was a cigar shape about eight feet long and about two feet in diameter and made out of a paper laminate set in some form of resin and about half an inch thick. We sorted through the cigar shaped tanks to find ones that were not damaged enough to affect our intended use. David, Dick and I wheeled our own selected tank back to their house and cut a hole about twenty four inches long and eighteen inches wide in the top middle, where the pipe connections were, with a rusty old wood saw. This made the tank into a canoe which, together with a paddle made from a split down skirting board, we

Chapter 9

wheeled down to the beach on our bicycles. The beach at Clacton at this time was theoretically inaccessible as it was covered by a scaffold tubing fence structure to prevent a German landing. However we determined boys were able to thread our canoes through and get to the water. Here we found a fundamental design fault. Being round in cross section, with our weight projecting vertically at the top, caused the canoe to immediately invert.

So we decided the canoes needed ballast, we roughly quarter filled the tank with sand which we then sat on and paddled. Of course this made the canoe very heavy and so while sitting in it we scooped out sand by hand until we had the minimum sand for stability. We then paddled around and always ended up by racing each other. Looking back on it I realise how dangerous this was, if we had turned over the sand would have dropped to the inside of the top, which had become the underside, trapping our legs so we would not be able to get out and certainly we would not have been able to right the canoe.

To finish canoeing we beached the canoe, shovelled out the sand until we could turn the canoe over and tip out the rest and then loaded the canoes onto our bicycles to go home. To return and go through the whole process the following day. Very exhausting work for boys.

I joined Collyer's School Drama Club when I was in the fourth form not because I was interested in drama but because my then best friends Eric Thompson and John Hempstead were members, and the drama club members used to go for an unsupervised week's camping at Stratford-upon-Avon to see the plays at the Shakespeare Memorial Theatre. To enter into the theatrical spirit of these weeks I used to wear a regimental Black Watch kilt bought from an army surplus store, sported a monocle and drank rough cider at a pub known on one side of its sign as The Black Swan and on the other side as The Dirty Duck. I spent the days punting on the River Avon – becoming very proficient which was a big help with the local girls.

In later years, married with family and dogs, I used to punt a great deal on the River Wey at Godalming/Guildford. We had many adventures including dog Benny stepping out of the boat onto a bed of floating algae thinking it was dry land and dog Bracken falling in near a weir. I only just managed to grab him as he was going down to certain death in the sluices at the bottom of the gates.

For the first holiday after Jane and I were married and when we had very little money, I wanted to introduce Jane to the pleasures of boating and chartered a Hillyard 2½ tonner based at Itchenor in Chichester Harbour for a week at a very low price.

A Hillyard 2½ tonner was a tiny wooden sailing boat with a little two berth cabin, they were built

Chapter 9

as affordable small boats by Hillyards at Littlehampton in the 1930s and were regarded as good starter boats.

The boat that we had chartered turned out to be a very worn example and in poor condition. The deck and coach roof planking had shrunk and in an attempt to seal it had long ago been covered with canvas and then painted: this had cracked with age. It was early in the year and the weather was poor. We sailed round Chichester Harbour for the first couple of days when it was cold and blowy. On the third day it got even colder and wetter. When it started to rain Jane, who understandably had not been enjoying the experience, got really upset and demanded to be set ashore. I agreed the whole thing was not much fun and proposed that after lunch we might go into Chichester and have a look round, have a reasonable tea and afterwards perhaps go to the cinema.

Our boat had a small rowing dinghy towed astern and after picking up a mooring in Itchenor channel we used the dinghy to row ashore to the Hard where there were two large chains for parking dinghies, to one of which we attached ours.

We came out of the cinema at about ten thirty and discovered it had been raining heavily. Our waterproofs were ex-army gas capes which were actually long coats with a bag in the back to be worn over full kit with a knapsack. We walked to the bus station and by sheer luck just caught the last bus to Itchenor. Itchenor village is just a few houses on either side of the road which goes straight down to the Hard and the water. The bus goes into Itchenor and turns round in the pub car park some way from the water, in order to return to Chichester.

Jane and I were the only people on the bus and when we got off the bus lights lit the road down to the water so that we set off without further thought. We had only gone a few yards when the bus lights went out as the bus turned round and we realised that not only were there no street lights but no houses were lit either. Itchenor residents being early to bed people. So there we were plunged into pitch darkness. I led Jane by the hand gingerly down the Hard and by feel and luck found our dinghy. The tide had gone down while we were away and was still ebbing strongly. We dragged the dinghy to the water but because there was no light missed the shingle of the Hard proper and reached the water through thick mud. We got aboard and I set off rowing only to realise once we had left the shore that I could not see a thing and I did not know exactly where our boat was anyway. Rowing up the channel against the strong tide and bumping repeatedly into moored boats which were not ours, eventually I found the stern of a boat which had an unusual projecting spar called a bumpkin which the Hillyard 2½ tonner had.

Chapter 9

I had found our boat by feel. Wet and exhausted we got aboard and could not wait to get into our bunks warm and dry. I opened the sliding hatch and lit the cabin lights to find that the roof had leaked badly and the two flock filled mattresses each had a substantial puddle in the middle. There was no way we could sleep on board and this time I fully agreed with Jane that we had got to get off the water. So we got back into the dinghy and I rowed back to the Hard by sense of feel. Actually, again I missed the hard part, this time on the other side and we both waded through the mud to the end of the road. By this time it was probably about twelve thirty and the only light we could see was a public telephone box much further up the street than where we had got off the bus. This held the possibility to get out of the rain so off to the phone box we went. When the two of us were huddled inside I read the advertisements on the back wall of the box, one of which was for a bed and breakfast house in Itchenor, so I rang the number without much hope. Much to my amazement a woman answered the phone and some lights came on just a short distance up the road. I explained our plight and the need for a bed and the woman took pity and said come along and she would take us in. We got to the lit up house and were welcomed in, given a cup of tea, shown to a very comfortable room and had our clothes taken away for drying. We had a long night's sleep and woke to a beautiful sunny morning and there were our clothes washed and ironed. We were given a splendid full English breakfast. I had explained the night before that we were very short of money and had been told not to worry and it could all be sorted out later. I got the very reasonable bill in the morning but even this was beyond my resources so it was agreed that I would send the money as soon as we got home.

Jane had had enough of boating so in spite of the lovely weather that morning we collected our things from the boat and went back home to Horsham. Looking back I think that episode killed boats and boating for all time with Jane, she never recovered and this explains her behavior in connection with boats thereafter.

In the late 1950s I got involved with C F Taylor, an entrepreneur at Wokingham, who made duct work and kitchen hoods for me when at Hadens but also had wide interests with several small factories. One was in the very early development stages of glass reinforced plastic (GRP) when the resin components were separate chemicals and very difficult to mix and control. Taylor had the contract to build the hull of a speedboat about eighteen feet in length to be fitted with a Dowty jet propulsion system – very advanced and state of the art. Due to the difficulties with the mixing about ten per cent of the hull mouldings were rejected as the resin had not set. This problem ranged from the whole thing dribbling out onto the floor when they opened the mould, to hulls

Chapter 9

with a couple of soft patches. The rejected hulls were piled up outside and periodically burnt. I managed to scrounge a reject hull which only had two very small soft spots, brought it home to Manor Cottage and kept it upside down on the grass in the front garden for many months.

At this time my friend Keith Gray had acquired an eight foot fibreglass dinghy and a Seahorse outboard motor which we used to tow down at low water to Shoreham, digging worm bait in the river on the way, and fish the rising tide outside the harbour. Our dress for these outings was ex-navy surplus duffel coats and normal black farmers Wellington boots, if we had fallen in we would have drowned, particularly Keith who could not swim. We used to get all sorts of advice from locals as to where to fish and one of these was about a mile straight out off the harbour entrance. One calm evening just as it was getting dark we went out to this spot, dropped our anchor, tipped up the outboard motor and started to fish. There were three merchant ships drifting, not underway, outside the harbour waiting for the tide to rise enough for them to get into the lock and into the inner basin. We passed close by one on the way out, so it was inshore of us about one hundred yards away. Another was about the same distance offshore away from us but some way off to one side. The third boat was a lot further out.

Of course, a little dinghy like ours had no ships lights and after a while when it was virtually dark we heard the engines start on the boat inshore of us and the boat put on a display of lights which meant nothing to us. At the same time the boat outside of us also put on some lights. The boat inside of us moved off slowly swinging round to aim for the harbour entrance and as it did so something like a two inch diameter round bar projecting from the water started some distance away to accelerate rapidly straight at our little boat. The hairs stood up on the back of my neck as my mind raced from submarine periscopes to sea monsters. We did not have time to move and Keith and I just sat there transfixed as the object passed about three feet from our stern and eventually stopped some thirty feet away to reveal itself as a wire rope cable, festooned with seaweed. It was a tow line from the ship inshore, with all the lights, to the ship further out with few lights and no engine noise which was being towed into Shoreham harbour. The cable had been lying on the seabed while the boats waited for the tide and when the towing boat started to move it tightened the cable which caused the catenary loop to rise up out of the water at speed to connect to the high bow of the towed vessel. We upped anchor and moved off very smartly and I decided to learn what ships lights indicated.

Keith Gray's brother heard about the fibreglass motorboat hull sitting upside down on the lawn of Manor Cottage and suggested a swap with a little sailing dinghy called a Runt which he had

Chapter 9

acquired. As it was unlikely that I should ever get around to sorting out the fibreglass hull a deal was done and the swap was completed. It turned out Runt was famous.

Photo 4: Runt

The America's Cup since its inception in 1870 is always competed for by big yachts and until 1983 had always been won by the Americans. Certainly before World War II all the British challengers for the America's Cup ended in ignominious failure. This upset the famous and leading British yacht designer of that period, Uffa Fox, who thought if we cannot beat the Americans in very big and expensive boats he would design and finance a small dinghy to race in America's smallest two man dinghy class that was for boats 12 feet in length. While Fox built one for himself and called it Runt he was approached by Peter Scott (sailor, naturalist, painter and son of Scott of the Antarctic) to build another for him. Uffa Fox did that and named it Squall and he and Peter Scott took them to the US and raced them with some success. This is all recorded in 'Uffa's Second Book'. Runt was brought back and became the prototype for National Twelve Class, a leading dinghy class designed by Uffa Fox which ultimately became an Olympic class.

Runt was a very shallow skimming dish hull with a heavy steel centre blade. I made a trailer and hitch from a Ferguson tractor part and fitted it to my Fiat 500 and towed Runt up and down to Shoreham Beach. Landing and recovery was very difficult and wetting. I got fed up with this. Why I did not join a yachting club I cannot recall, in any case I eventually sold Runt.

For some years I had no time for boats as I was building Severals House, but then I came across (through a contact with Miles Aircraft at Shoreham with whom I sat on a committee) a

Chapter 9

mould for a fibreglass twenty eight foot American designed boat called Controversy, which I bought at scrap price. I brought the mould up to Severals House in several pieces on a borrowed trailer. I redesigned the deck and cabin top to a more English version and advertised for an amateur group to build the boat themselves. I got five replies one of which was from Dick Haines who was a main board director of Plessey's and who had a farm half a mile up the road from our house. The group built a mould for my redesigned superstructure in a semi derelict barn on Dick Haines farm. We decided that moulding actual boats was beyond us so we had five boats moulded by a professional firm on Ford Aerodrome, one for each of us.

I brought my hull/deck unit home and put it in the back garden at Severals. We sold the moulds to another group based on the River Ribble in Yorkshire and never heard any more about them.

There were no facilities to fit out the boat at home and so after some years I took it down to the BATHRAD factory and worked on it there for some time. Eventually it was finished, named Sevorg (Groves spelt backwards) and launched at Shoreham Lady Bee yard. This was a terrible derelict place where I dropped the mast and smuts from the power station ruined the sails and access to the sea was through the big ship lock which only opened occasionally.

Photo 5: Sevorg

I decided to move to Chichester where we put Sevorg in the Yacht Basin (as it was then called).

The boat did not sail well. My design of keel was quite wrong, it had excessive weather helm which meant that in a strong gust of wind I was unable to prevent the boat screwing up into the wind. I had a chat with the yacht design department at Southampton University who recommended the removal of the front section of the keel, which was six inch thick cast iron, involving a cut about five feet long. This I

Chapter 9

undertook in the winter in the car park of Chichester Yacht Basin. I originally engaged an engineering firm to cut this keel part off but they found it beyond them but wanted money, which I declined to pay. They then drilled three half-inch diameter holes in the hull below the waterline and plugged them with blue plasticine to match the anti fouling. Fortunately I found these before the boat was returned to the water. But I still had to cut a piece off the keel.

I ended up by bolting a piece of steel plate to the side of the keel, hiring for one weekend a big magnetic pillar drill and drilling a series of holes along the cut line to make perforations. On a bitterly cold weekend John Woodhatch and I spent all day both Saturday and Sunday drilling these holes and by Sunday night had finished, but the piece had not dropped off. Exhausted, I lost my temper and gave the keel an almighty blow with a sledgehammer whereupon the front piece dropped off. It weighed 300lbs. I had intended to grind out the half holes left at the front of the keel but found this to be virtually impossible so I made up a round nosing for the keel out of GRP resin and woodchips which worked fine and when painted was undetectable.

The next spring the boat sailed fine, but revealed my sailing skills to be inadequate so I enrolled on a practical course with Bosham Sea School whose instructor was Wally Naismith with whom I got on very well. I completed the course at

Day Skipper level and after gaining a good deal of experience sailing Sevorg that summer, at Wally's suggestion, I returned in the autumn to obtain my Yachtmaster Practical Certificate. Wally suggested I might come the following year and do a bit of instructing on weekend courses to give him a bit of time off during the mid-summer busy period.

So I obtained progressively all the RYA Instructor qualifications ending up with the full bag, Yachtmaster Ocean and Yachtmaster Powerboat.

Forest Boys School in Horsham asked me to teach the RYA Shorebased Syllabus one evening each week for the school year on a two year cycle – Competent Crew/Day Skipper one year with Yachtmaster the following year. I took this on. These courses were a great success, generally over subscribed. I then taught in Horsham for over twenty years followed by twelve years in Selsey after I retired, and for some years in Haywards Heath until I got fed up with the winter night journeys.

At the end of my first year a number of students asked me to take them on the week's practical sailing course so I approached Bosham Sea School, for whom I had already agreed to do the odd weekend. They were only too happy for me to join them to do week courses for my students and afterwards the overflow of their normal applicants. So I became a professional sailing instructor, albeit part time but earning

Chapter 9

modest money with which to finance my private sailing activities. A good set up.

Through my teaching, particularly the practical sailing, I met many nice people and made a number of lasting friends. I also had a number of interesting experiences, some I think worth telling.

For RYA courses the instructor/student ratio is 1 to 5 and we sailed standard production boats around 32 ft in length as examples of what the students might eventually buy for themselves. The courses I ran were mixed ability courses that ranged from beginners to Yachtmaster candidates. Over the years I met a huge range of people types, most I liked and some I didn't take to at all.

One recollection I have is of a chap named Brooks, a successful fan manufacturer. Elderly Brooks had a large number of grandchildren. When the oldest of these grandchildren reached the age of eighteen Brooks had puzzled over what unusual present to give and had settled on a week's dinghy sailing course with Bosham Sea School. This had gone down very well and in following years became the standard eighteenth birthday present for all of his grandchildren. So Bosham Sea School had had a lot of business from Brooks over the years and as a token of their gratitude Basil Goodman, who ran Bosham Sea School, offered Brooks and his wife a complimentary weekend sailing with one of my courses.

Brooks and his wife arrived in an enormous chauffer driven Rolls Royce from which Brooks alighted wearing golfing clothes, plus four trousers, check socks and metal studded shoes. His chauffer got eight large matching fitted pigskin cases from the car boot. I said to Brooks that particularly he could not wear those shoes on a boat and that while we might be able to accommodate one of his suitcases the other seven would have to stay behind. Brooks took it all in good part saying that he had brought a lot of stuff because he didn't know whether we dressed for dinner! I put him right on that one and suggested that he went to the School shop and bought a sweater, jeans and a pair of sailing plimsolls. This he did and took one suitcase upstairs to the flat over the School to change. Eventually he came down properly dressed and off we all went to the boat. Brooks said at the outset that he didn't want to learn to sail but he and his wife just wanted to come along for the ride. Fair enough.

On the Saturday we did a bit of sail training off Chichester and set off down the Solent to stay the night, which would normally have been in Cowes. However, it happened to be the weekend of Cowes Week Regatta when Cowes was choked with boats so we were to sail on west to Lymington.

As we passed Cowes we came to the Royal Yacht Britannia anchored outside the harbour in Cowes Roads, very smart in the sunshine with three enormous royal pennant flags flying. Brooks

Chapter 9

asked me what the boat was and when I told him he was very excited apparently being a lifelong Royal fan.

On the Sunday morning we got up early to catch the tide and pass Cowes at about ten o'clock when all the boats were coming out to race so that there was this huge mass of boats gilling about in the Solent right across our course. The student steering lost his nerve and so I took the helm as we plunged in among these boats.

I waved and said "good morning" to any boats passing close to us. A very large ocean racer, pale green in colour with a flush deck, (no cabin top) with a crew of about fourteen all dressed in pale green uniforms, except for one man at the stern steering with an enormous wheel, and wearing a bright red pullover, came sliding by going in the opposite direction and very close to us. The man in the red pullover was the Duke of Edinburgh for whom an ordinary greeting was not appropriate so I called out "Good Morning, Sir" The addition of the word Sir caused Brooks to look up straight at the Duke passing some twenty feet from him, just as the Duke responded to my greeting by saying "Good Morning" with the Royal stiff bent-arm wave and slight bow. Brooks was gob-smacked and talked continuously about his royal encounter all the way back to Chichester and the end of the course.

After I dropped the crew off I had to go to the School to put in a sail for repair. When I went in

Basil Goodman asked me how Brooks had enjoyed his week end. I told him about the royal encounter. I then went into the little screened off office where I was out of sight to write out a note for the sail repair. While there I heard the front door open and Brooks saying he had come back for the suitcase he had forgotten and had left upstairs. Basil responded by asking whether he had enjoyed the weekend and before Brooks could complete the deep breath he was taking to reply, Basil said "Did the Duke of Edinburgh say Good Morning to you, because we did ask him to see Colin outside Cowes this morning?" Brooks just gasped and said "Yes". The standing of Bosham Sea School held top spot for Brooks for the rest of his life.

Occasionally these sailing courses altered people's lives. An example is that I took a five day course one year at Easter, the beginning of the sailing season. The awaiting student crew were four fellows and a dapper middle aged lady named Gwen, who was looking decidedly apprehensive and liable to escape back home any minute. I took her under my wing, explained how the course worked which reassured her. We went sailing and Gwen settled down and began to take part, she enjoyed herself and proved to be very competent. Towards the end of the week I was chatting to Gwen after dinner and after she told me how much she had enjoyed the week so I asked her how she had managed to enrol for a sailing

Chapter 9

course. She then told me. She was a spinster and Senior Matron at St. Thomas' Hospital, London. She lived in the nurses' hostel although she owned a house in Sidcup to which she occasionally escaped. She got quite a lot of holidays each year and being a single person had never found a holiday she enjoyed. She had progressed through Mediterranean beach holidays to pony trekking the Pyrenees without finding anything she wanted to do again. Many years before she had been at Nurses Training College with a fellow student who was disliked by everybody and for whom Gwen felt sorry and was thus kinder to her than anyone else. So this fellow student regarded Gwen as her best friend. After College these two nurses went their separate ways, the other nurse ended up at The Radcliffe in Oxford, Gwen at St. Thomas'. They kept in contact only by Christmas cards but always the card Gwen got included a request that the two of them should holiday together. Gwen had resisted until the summer before she came on my course.

She agreed to go with her "friend" on a two week coach trip to tour the Greek antiquities and ruins organized by the South Oxford Ladies Archaeological Society. Gwen turned up at Victoria Coach Station and joined the Greek coach driven by a Greek driver for this two week outing with a coach full of women. The journey to Greece was a nightmare – the driver got drunk every lunch time and Gwen's companion talked constantly about nothing in particular.

Gwen remembered nothing of the actual holiday except climbing endless steps in very hot sunshine.

By the time the coach was on the cross channel ferry coming home Gwen had had enough and left the party to complete the journey on her own by train. On the train with nothing to do Gwen found a copy of Yachting World that somebody had left behind. She leafed through it and found Bosham Sea School's advertisement. Reeling from her latest awful holiday she completed the application form for the following year, posted it when she got to London and promptly forgot all about it.

When sent her joining instructions the following spring she was on the verge of not coming but plucked up her courage to give it a try. Hence her nervousness at the start.

She had thoroughly enjoyed the course. Living her precise and ordered normal life she had no experience of the free and easy ways of small boat pleasure sailing. She was captivated and tried to book the next level course with me there and then. I explained that she should get some sailing experience to benefit from the next level course. She asked me how she could do that. I said that I was awarding her a Competent Crew Certificate at the end of my course and with that she should join a Yacht Club and put a notice on the board

Chapter 9

offering herself as Crew. She looked a little doubtful about this.

The course ended and I was amused to see Gwen, who was probably about fifty years old, picked up by her mother and father in a Morris Minor Traveller. I promptly forgot Gwen and went on to other things.

The following Christmas among a great many cards received at home was one from Gwen which brought her to mind again. This was a large card with the inside and back covered in close writing. From this I found that Gwen had joined a sailing club near her Sidcup house and had sailed with several people until meeting up with a widowed doctor, a boat owning club member, with whom she had forged a strong bond. They had sailed cross channel five times that year and were planning a three week trip to the Baltic for the following summer. She ended by thanking me for introducing her to a new life!!

While practical instructing with Bosham Sea School the School and I featured in a television holiday programme called "Wish You Were Here". I did not exhibit star quality. The video tape is still around somewhere at home.

One other thing from my teaching practical sailing which is of general interest is the story of Stugeron as I know it.

As can be imagined sea sickness is a very real problem for a sailing school. If you had one person in your crew of five who was seriously sea sick you had to return to port and ruin the day for everybody. In my early days the school boat used to carry a selection of sea sickness remedies none of which seemed very effective. These drugs were normal over-the-counter remedies sold in chemist's shops. They were the post war civilian version of drugs developed by boffins during the war to help troops crossing the Channel on the D Day invasion of France. These drugs were either Avomines or Hyoscyamines which are nerve depressants which theoretically damp you down so you are not sensitive to sea sickness. In my experience these drugs do not work very well and render the taker pretty well comatose, so they were definitely not the answer to sea sickness for a sailing school.

There were two young doctors working together in a hospital somewhere on the east coast who jointly bought a yacht and took up sailing only to find that they were both prone to sea sickness. They tried the usual remedies but predictably found them of little use. Thinking about this with their medical training they thought that medical research advances in the treatment of travel sickness, of which sea sickness is one form, must now be possible. So using their hospital credentials they wrote to every transport organization that they could think of, ferry companies, airlines, etc, asking for incidents of travel sickness to passenger miles/hours travelled. They, as most people, thought the worst

Chapter 9

would be cross channel ferries in bad weather. The results of the survey were an unexpected revelation. The highest incidence of travel sickness was on a hovercraft. It was not the pitching and rolling of a ferry ship that caused the problem but the harsh jiggling ride of a hovercraft in even calm conditions.

Puzzling over this result the doctors sought the next means of travel that gave a ride most like a hover craft and found that this was riding a normal bicycle. There had never been a case of travel sickness on a bicycle. So it was not the physical motion that caused the problem. In order to stay upright when riding a bicycle you are subconsciously reading the horizon with your eyes and your brain combines that information with that from the semi-circular canals in your ears, the balance organs, and maintains the equilibrium of the body and keep it comfortable. However, with a hover craft underway the spray obscures the windows so the occupants cannot read the horizon, although their bodies are undergoing the same motion as they would on bicycles, and they become disorientated and travel sick. This effect can often be felt by a car passenger when reading a map. They are perfectly alright all the time they are looking out of the windows at the horizon but when the driver asks them to look down to read a map they feel sick.

Hence, concluded the doctors, the source of the problem is with the inner ear balance organs.

There is a well known but relatively rare disease, Meniere's Disease, which affects the inner ear organs and causes sufferers to lose their balance. This is treated by a drug sold under the name of Stugeron produced in limited numbers by only one company. The doctors tried Stugeron on themselves and found it very effective. Thinking that all their research work had cured them psychologically, they tried Stugeron on all their friends they could get to sail with them. Again they found Stugeron effective. Next they wrote to the yachting press and asked readers to take part in a field trial with free issue Stugeron. This offer was taken up by readers of Yachting Monthly with the results published in the bumper Christmas issue. These results were virtually one hundred per cent positive. The production of Stugeron was increased many times and the drug was packaged and sold as a travel sickness preventative. Taken as instructed I have found Stugeron entirely effective and it completely eliminated sea sickness from the school's sailing courses. As they say "Since then I have used no other".

Sea sickness remedies – but not Stugeron – were responsible for the only significant injury to anyone during the some twenty five years I taught practical sailing. At the very start of one sailing season I collected five students for a week's course. These included a middle aged American couple, the husband was a normal person but the wife was like the cartoon character Marge

Chapter 9

Simpson. She had a lot of permanently waved blue hair and massively framed upswept spectacles with imitation diamonds embedded all round. Her worst feature was her voice: twangy mid-USA that sounded like sawing a piece of wood and hitting a nail. It was immediately apparent that this American couple were not sailors. At the start of every course I had a small chat setting out the boat rules and asking if anyone wanted Stugeron, explaining how the course ran, where the safety equipment was kept, etc., and always ending up by asking if anyone had a medical condition that I ought to know about. In this instance nobody said anything. We turned in for the night, the American couple in the two-berth fore cabin.

In the morning we set about breakfast which the American woman said she did not eat but would like an empty cereal bowl and a cup of coffee. She took the bowl went into the forecabin and after a short delay came back to the table with at least twenty different pills and capsules in the bowl which she proceeded to eat one by one with mouthfuls of coffee. These were obviously some form of medication about which she had said nothing the previous night. I could not berate this woman in front of the others but after breakfast when she had retired back to the fore cabin I took her husband outside and asked him what was going on with all these pills. He said "Oh, they are her sea sickness remedies" – I asked him to explain. It turned out that this chap had had a very successful domestic oil fired central heating air furnace installing business in the geographic centre of USA at the most distant point from the sea in the whole country. Apparently a couple of years before he was with me, he went on a boys only holiday with local business chums for a two week self sail charter holiday on one of the Great Lakes. This experience captivated him so much that he returned home to tell his wife that he was going to sell his business and house and they were going to retire to sail round the world. Just like that – and his wife had never even seen the sea. He thought that British yachts were better than American ones and he found out that Britain had lots of sailing schools so to start his world sailing they would come to England, do a course with Bosham Sea School, buy a boat and set off. To ease his wife into this new life style they had agreed to tour from their home town to see something of the country they were leaving to New York and then a holiday in London before starting on their big adventure.

All their landlubber friends in their home town, probably jealous of their adventure, bombarded the wife with terrible tales about sea sickness. She went to every chemist, pharmacy and mail order drug supplier and bought their recommended sea sickness remedy, and continued with this during their stay in New York

Chapter 9

and subsequently in London. It was these pills she had taken at breakfast.

I told her husband that it was very unwise to take such a cocktail of drugs as they were almost certainly the old nerve depressant types, but he said she will not listen and will persist. As I anticipated this woman emerged for the first day's sail only semi-conscious saying that she would just sit in the cockpit and spectate. She did not want to learn to sail. After a while she began to feel guilty for sitting there alone doing nothing while everyone else was working the boat as the weather was a bit rough. She knew that Brits like their tea so she took on the role of tea-maker which she offered to do about every half an hour.

On the penultimate day of the course we sailed back to the Solent from Poole in very heavy weather with rough seas which meant that we had to all stay in the cockpit with the hatches shut and no tea could be produced until we had passed through Hurst Narrows and were in the Solent. In these calmer conditions we accepted the American woman's offer to make tea. I opened the hatch and she went down to the galley immediately below and put the kettle on. A little while later we heard the kettle whistle and I looked down the hatch to take the cups of tea from her and pass them round. However, what I saw was her with her hand open and with the kettle of boiling water hanging down, and when she tried to put it back down upon the stove it came back up with her hand. She was not reacting to this but merely blankly staring at her hand.

Realising that something was badly wrong I jumped down, got a cloth, held the kettle and peeled her hand off the kettle handle. This uninsulated metal kettle handle for styling reasons extended from the top down the back of the kettle in a curve to the base. The kettle must have been misplaced on the gas burner so that the flame had played on the end of the handle while the kettle was heating up. The result was that when the woman picked up the kettle to make the first mug of tea the near red hot handle had burnt the palm of her hand. Now normally, even before your hand touches it, metal that hot would cause a reflex action withdrawal. Even if you had got as far as touching the handle you would certainly not have held on to it as this woman did. She had a deep wound groove across her palm in which I could see the tendons of her fingers. There was virtually no bleeding, I think the hot handle had actually cauterized the wound. This was a terrible injury but she showed no signs of being in pain, she just looked blankly at her hand.

Fortunately we had a clean tea towel in which I wrapped her hand and we drove the boat straight into Lymington Marina. With both of us in full wet weather gear and safety harnesses jingling like shire horses, I took the woman to the nearest doctor in the High Street. He was closed for tea

Chapter 9

but I knocked him up and grudgingly he took the woman into his surgery. He asked me in after a while and said that she certainly had this fearful burn. I pointed out that the course finished in Chichester the following day. He bound up the hand to the size of a football and put the arm in a sling.

He said the extraordinary thing was that this woman showed no signs of being in pain or any distress and I told him about the multiple sea sickness medication. "That explains it" he said, "but if those affects wear off she will be in agony – I will give you some morphine injections to give her should this happen." I said I didn't know how to inject morphine. He said "You do it like this." He got a hypodermic syringe and jabbed it into an orange. He gave me the syringe with three lots of morphine. We returned to the boat, persuaded the woman to bed and fortunately I did not have to use the morphine. Back in Chichester her husband set off with her to the American Hospital in London after thanking me for making him realise that, irrespective of the injury to his wife, his idea of immediately setting off to sail the world was a non-starter. They would be going back to the USA to rethink the whole thing!

I was in great demand, in fact I could have taught full-time. I did sail a lot as a professional instructor, mostly at weekends, but also about four or five five-day courses each year mostly for

Bosham Sea School during which I met a lot of people, some of whom became long standing friends. Among these was Tony Mack who, with his wife Sally, came to my classes in Haywards Heath. Tony was into racing which had not previously interested me but we bought jointly a day racing sailing keelboat called a Squib from famous Peter Nicholson, a member of the Nicholson family who had a big boatyard and marina in Gosport, and who was a regular winner of big yacht races,. We sailed the Squib in fleet races based on Brighton Marina for one season. Getting in and out of the Marina without an engine tuned our sailing skills.

Tony enjoyed racing so much he bought a Contessa 33 and with him as skipper, me as navigator and three or four chums from East Grinstead Rugby Club as crew we raced this boat with increasing success for a couple of years. Flushed with these successes Tony bought first a Danish 34ft X-Yacht followed a couple of years later by a 38ft flat out racing X-Yacht to progress into the very top echelon of British yacht racing. All Tony's racing yachts had the name McFly. I and the nucleus of the original crew remained augmented by additions over the years to ultimately number twelve. We did very well winning many prizes and I believe at one time we were under consideration for the one yacht of our size in the British Admirals Cup team for this

Chapter 9

prestigious international yacht race, although we were not ultimately selected.

Photo 6: McFly – top level yacht racing

During the foregoing period Tony had occasionally added a full time professional hot shot crew member to obtain advice on individual aspects of our racing, sail setting was one while another was race tactics. Then, during one off season, Tony – keen for more success, took on permanently for the following season a team of three professional yacht racers, one of whom was a navigator. This made me redundant so I resigned and raced no more. I did not in the least mind as the whole racing thing was getting far too intense for my taste, I sailed for pleasure and I didn't need the intense pressure involved with this top level racing. Best leave it to the professionals.

One year while I was still in the crew Tony chartered a yacht in the British Virgin Islands and the whole crew went for a week to race in the Tortola BVI Regatta. We won against a large fleet of American yachts. Tony and all the old original crew members remain firm friends and we have a very alcoholic reunion every year.

I might mention that Tony's personal life was just as successful as his yacht racing as during the period I was sailing with him he went from running a small air charter company, started for the Berlin Air Lift of 1948, which he inherited from his father, through to going public, with the company renamed Air Partner. It became the biggest air charter company in the world with offices all over the world. Tony is now semi-retired Chairman and worth umpteen millions. Fortunately my father's trust fund has for some years had a few shares in Tony's company.

However, I was hooked on sailing and, as my planned retirement from my Consulting Practice was not that many years away, I decided to build a boat capable of being lived on and to sail round the world when I retired. I carried out intensive research, read everything available and settled on a Reve Des Seychelles design for a thirty eight foot six inches long by twelve foot six inch beam and five foot seven inch draft design by Group Finot in

Chapter 9

Paris which I found in wonderful book 'The Proper Yacht' by Arthur Beiser.

To involve Jane in the project I took her to Paris to discuss and buy the designs from Group Finot. These designs were for building in steel or aluminium and to save on maintenance I decided on aluminium. There were not many British builders in aluminium but I eventually settled on a firm, Metalair Marine, at Long Sutton near Kings Lynn, Norfolk on the East Coast. This set up was a new off-shoot of Metalair who made dry bulkers, which are aluminium pressurized powder carriers on lorries.

After all sorts of problems I eventually got the hull and deck unit built and brought back to Horsham for me to fit out and finish off. This was a big boat by the standard of those days, it required a police escort all the way from Long Sutton to Horsham and could only pass through London at night. Eventually I squeezed it into Grove House office car park alongside No 3. I built a scaffold around the boat and stored materials on the empty first floor of the adjoining No 3. John Woodhatch and I working one weekday and at weekends and eventually finished the boat except for the painting which was done by a yard on Hayling Island managed by Wally Naismith my chum from Bosham Sea School. During the three year building process Jane had shown no interest whatever in the project even to the point of declining to discuss the colour scheme.

Photo 7: Upshot

The boat was eventually finished and I decided to have a proper launching ceremony using the 'travel lift' at Chichester Yacht Basin, with lunch at the yacht club afterwards. I issued formal invitations to the few friends who had been

Chapter 9

involved in the building. The chosen day was very cold early April and the yard had to be at a virtual standstill at 11 o'clock so the ceremony could take place. The launch was to be by Buff Gibbings a friend of Jane's but a keen experienced sailor. We stood about in the cold with the boat in slings in the travel lift for about an hour waiting for Jane who eventually arrived without an apology. A graphic demonstration on how keen she was on the whole idea of retiring on a boat.

The boat was named Upshot and launched successfully.

The boat sailed beautifully and was a complete success. I sailed it with friends and occasionally Rachel for about three years trying the while to get Jane interested, without success. It came to a head when we had sailed round from Chichester to Portsmouth to stay on the boat for a weekend steam boat rally. This Jane seemed to enjoy but coming out of Portsmouth under power on the Monday on a beautiful calm sunny morning to come back to Chichester, I asked Jane to steer with me standing by, she took the helm for about three minutes and then let go and collapsed sobbing onto the cockpit seat saying she could not do it, she was too frightened. That was the end of retiring and sailing round the world together.

It was a waste of a beautiful boat to just use it for occasional weekends so I sold it to a young man and his father. The young man was an officer in the Gurkhas and had arranged a year's sabbatical on half pay to sail round the world with his wife – the father was putting up half the money to purchase the boat. He sailed away

Photo 8: Upshot off Tahiti

Chapter 9

without modifying the boat in any way and I got occasional postcards reporting progress. The last one was about a year later from Tahiti saying that the trip was such a success that he had resigned from the army and would not be coming back for some time.

About two years later I was at the Southampton Boat Show when I was accosted by a young chap with the deepest tan I had ever seen who greeted me like a long lost brother. When I asked who he was he explained he was the lad that bought Upshot. The boat had performed faultlessly and was an unqualified success. He had come home to have the boat painted and have some new sails made before setting off with his wife to go round again.

He wrote a series of articles for Yachting World magazine during his second trip. After he came back the second time his father and mother said it was their turn and they set off to cruise round the world. I never heard any more from them but it does seem to prove that the design of the boat was about right and the build and fit out was to the right standards.

With the demise of my plan to retire and sail with Jane around the world and with Jane's apparent mild interest in elegant freshwater steamboats, I decided to build a steam launch on which we could sleep. After much searching I was unable to find a suitable period hull so I had moulded with epoxy resin a pretty estuary cruising hull called a Pelican. I acquired a 1932 Drysdale single cylinder 8 IHP steam engine, originally a ship's pumping engine hence no reverse. I did not want to modify an original engine to fit reverse so I went looking for a steering and reversing device that I had seen mentioned in old books called a Kitchen rudder, patented by Admiral Kitchen in the 1920s and used only on some pinnaces by the Royal Navy between the wars. A Kitchen rudder and its operating gear were all bronze castings and every ship breakers I contacted over a period of about two years said that they had all been melted down during World War II.

By arrangement I went to The National Maritime Museum at Greenwich and was allowed to search their naval ships' record drawings – a fantastic archive of ships' designs going back to Henry VIII's time. There I found several drawings including Kitchen rudders which the museum copied and gave to me so I now knew what I was looking for. Then, by chance, I called into Belsize Boatyard a very old breakers yard in Southampton. They had a Kitchen rudder on a rotting hulk lying in the mud outside the yard which they said I could buy but only if I got it off the hull because they could not spare the time. I went down with tools and with a little unofficial help, in exchange for cash, from some of the yard lads I got the Kitchen rudder, weighing about 300lbs, off and loaded it into my trailer. I was

Chapter 9

disappointed that the whole thing was painted naval grey and the underwater parts had been anti-fouled, the whole thing showing no sign of being bronze as I had hoped. However when I got it offloaded at home and attacked it with a chisel I found the paint to be over 4mm thick onto bronze. It took a lot work to remove all of the paint.

A Kitchen rudder consists of two curved plates around the propeller. These plates are moved sideways by the tiller to steer the boat and can be closed behind the propeller to achieve reverse. The manual reversing mechanism was incorporated into the tiller which did not suit my design for a forward control steam launch, so I designed and build a remote control hydraulic system to operate the Kitchen rudder which worked just fine.

I built an aluminium saloon launch superstructure for the hull and with help from John Woodhatch I fitted out the hull to a high standard, using teak to provide two berths and seating for up to eight.

I originally fitted a boiler bought from an amateur builder but found that it did not produce enough steam to run my engine, then I came across articles about 'flash steam' monotube boilers, that is a boiler without steam storage and thus much safer. I built a monotube boiler to a period French Serpollet design using three hundred feet of half inch bore stainless steel tube and fired on paraffin with a period 'Lune Valley' burner which I had built. The final boat came out looking very good and the whole launch eventually worked just fine. It was called Grampus.

Photo 9: Grampus – Steam Launch

However, Jane showed no interest whatever in the project and, after having the steam launch in the water in Chichester Yacht Basin for a few years with very little use, I brought it home and put it up for sale. At the time of writing it is still unsold.

Sometime before this steam launch activity Rachel, who had been catering on boats in the French Riviera for a couple of years, was getting married to Iain and was worrying about getting somewhere to live. I came across a chap called Jack Barr whom I first met when he was Managing Director of Lintotts, an engineering firm

Chapter 9

opposite my office at Grove House, Foundry Lane. Jack Barr was then managing director of F.B.M. a serious ship building yard in Cowes, Isle of Wight.

F.B.M. had an order for six sixty foot steel motorboats for use as pilot boats for the Nigerian Government. They had built and delivered two boats but the Nigerians would not pay for them, so F.B.M. cancelled the contract and stopped work on the third boat for which they had completed the hull.

Photo 10: Sixty Six Foot Motor Yacht

Jack Barr agreed to sell me that hull at a knock down price. I designed a simple but smart current style superstructure with accommodation for up to twelve guests with the idea of presenting the completed boat to Rachel as a wedding present for her and Iain to live aboard on the French Riviera and earn a living by running charters, Iain skippering and Rachel catering, in the Mediterranean. I sought a builder to complete the boat to my designs and settled on a firm, Sims Leppard, conveniently on the Isle of Wight. The hull was towed from Cowes to Newport, lifted out and set ashore on land beside the approach road to Island Harbour Marina, for Sims Leppard to do their stuff.

I had found three Gardner 6LX diesel engines which had come from the three launches kept by the Port of London authority for Royal and VIP use. These engines were each about the size of a mini car and had certainly been used, so I rang Gardners in Manchester and spoke to a son of the Gardner family who was then running a firm to recondition Gardner engines. Because of the sort of firm Gardners were, he knew of the engines and had a record of the hours they had operated for. He said they certainly didn't need any rebuilding or overhaul, they were hardly run in. He said: "We don't overhaul engines until they have done a million miles in a bus or the equivalent hours in a boat." This I found astonishing.

Sims Leppard started work and made good progress for a couple of months and then stopped work without any explanation. It transpired the Isle of Wight Planning Office had placed a removal order on the boat, as Sims Leppard had not bothered to get planning permission.

Chapter 9

Simultaneously Sims Leppard went into liquidation. I had to pay to have the boat moved back to Newport, put back in the water and towed downriver to temporary and expensive storage at Souters Yard in Cowes. From there I had the boat towed by a professional towage firm to Hayling Island Yacht Company marina and there stored ashore until I could work out what to do with it. Rachel and Iain got married in the meantime and bought a house in Brighton. So the boat idea became redundant. I advertised the hull, part superstructure and engines for sale and sold the whole kit to a firm who serviced North Sea oil rigs and needed to transport men and equipment out from the mainland and back. They were very pleased with their purchase and not long afterwards I saw my boat in use in a television news story.

After the steam launch saga it was obvious that Jane was not interested in anything to do with boats, so I set about acquiring a boat I could sail alone in Chichester Harbour and along the south coast. I selected a twenty six foot long Cat Ketch hard chine centre plate design by Bruce Kirby, famous designer of worldwide Lazer dinghies. This boat is designated a "Norwalk Island Sharpie". With some help I turned to and built this boat in plywood using the "West" epoxy saturation technique. It turned out to be a very pretty, racy little boat which sailed well and which I named Bella in honour of my first German Shepherd dog.

Unfortunately, I altered the original design of the centre plate thinking that it was too light and made mine out of steel plate. The weight of the resultant plate was excessive and I never resolved the matter of raising the plate sensibly. After struggling with it for a few years I brought it home to modify the centre plate but have been too busy with other things to do it, the boat remains here at time of writing.

Chapter 10 - Cars and bikes – part 1

I have been interested in cars since I was about five years old. In those days before WW2 cars were rare things. Our house Cheslyn in Highams Park was at one end of a terrace of five houses, the house at the opposite end belonged to the Jenkins family and had the only garage in the area. The Jenkins parents were much older than my mother and father and they had two grown up sons, one of whom, David, had a Morris 8 Tourer. As far as I recall the only car in the district.

One hot summer's Sunday morning in those gentler times I was kitted out in very short shorts and a sun hat and walked up to the Jenkins house because I had seen the Morris 8 with its roof down being polished in the driveway. I stood and stared fascinated by the car in the sun. David Jenkins saw me and said he was going to get petrol and would I like to come, of course I jumped at the chance and David helped me into the passenger seat. The upholstery was leather on which the sun had been beating and was so hot it burnt the backs of my legs, but I said nothing, held back the tears and off we went for the couple of miles up to Woodford New Road where David bought petrol from a hand operated petrol pump with the hose on the end of a swing out arm to reach the car across the pavement. I stayed in the car shielding the seat from the sun and enjoyed the ride home much more. I was hooked on cars.

One Saturday, probably a couple of years later, I was with my parents and sister on a family shopping outing walking up towards Woodford Green where we passed a small parade of shops set back from the normal pavement by a paved strip on which some of the shops displayed their wares. One of these shops sold radios and outside they had a demonstration of one of the very first television sets. A plywood box with a screen about six inches across. Out of curiosity my parents stopped, amongst several other people, to look at this strange phenomenon which was showing pictures from Brooklands Motor Race Circuit at Weybridge in Surrey. The pictures were very flickery and indistinct and showed John Cobb in his Napier-Railton on the Brooklands banking. The camera was fixed so all you saw was this car, apparently leaning forward at a seemingly impossible angle, flash across the screen periodically.

I was captivated and eventually had to be dragged away to do the shopping we had come for.

That car, the Napier-Railton still exists and is on permanent display at Brooklands Museum and occasionally comes out on demonstrations. This episode was so deeply etched in my memory that some ten years later I did a linocut picture of that car on the Brooklands banking which was

Chapter 10

sufficiently good to be published in the Collyers School annual magazine.

At Collyers School during the War there were virtually no cars around due to petrol shortages and other wartime restrictions. However, two of the masters had cars which they were able to use occasionally. One of these was Rees, the master who taught maths to the upper school and issued lots of detentions which required staying late after school. The punishment duty consisted of, as I recall, dissolving moth balls in sheep dip in a big tin bath and this concoction Rees used to power his car. The other car was owned by Henderson a general dogs-body Master, who must have had some official part-time job because he had an Austin 10 car with a huge gas bag on the roof. The engine would have been converted to run on town gas, the normal domestic gas which was a by-product of making coke in the gasworks that were in every town. This car was appallingly slow as we were easily able to overtake it on bicycles even on level roads.

I had a school chum named Davis who lived with his Spanish mother in a flat in Bishopric Court in Horsham and who had a small motorcycle in pieces which I persuaded him to sell me for £1. I took this bike home in sacks on my bicycle in three journeys. It turned out to be a 1914 Omega 2 stroke of about 200cc with beaded edge (high pressure) tyres, belt drive two speed gears, no clutch, and a push start. Omegas were

Cars and Bikes - Part 1

sold by Gamages, a cut price department store in London.

I was sixteen years old, too young to get a driving license, and I only had my father's tools, kept in a box under the sink, consisting mainly of a bent screwdriver, a pair of pincers, an adjustable spanner and a hammer. But by the end of the 1947 school summer holidays I had managed to get the parts assembled to look like a motorcycle and spent every evening for about a week pushing the thing up and down Cambridge Road where we then lived, attempting to start the engine, without success. Finally, a man who lived in New Street on the corner of Cambridge Road, who had watched me from his garden shed and taken pity on me, came out to help. His name was Ted Jervis and he became a friend for the next some forty years. Ted said I had the ignition timing wrong – I did not even know what ignition timing was – he reset the timing and I got the bike to run. During the following winter I used to ride around the extensive allotments in Clarence Road at the other end of Cambridge Road. I obtained a provisional licence on my seventeenth birthday and then used the bike on the road. There were only two people in Collyer's School who had motorcycles, the other one was Baldy Leppard with a new 350cc NSU – of whom more later – and me with the Omega, the subject of much derision being a very old machine.

Chapter 10

I decided to exploit the age thing and acquired at a farm auction sale a magnificent ankle length beige leather Victorian motoring coat which I wore with a long scarf, cap back to front, huge gauntlet gloves and Victorian round goggles.

This bike was never reliable and the belt slipped badly in wet weather, so a permanent accessory was carrying a baked bean tin containing rosin dissolved in meths which was poured onto the belt about every mile in wet weather to reduce the belt slip.

For some reason I cannot now recall, I ventured as far as Brighton on this bike, there was probably some girl I went to see. Anyway during the day in Brighton I saw some large oranges for sale – which, bearing in mind we still had wartime rationing, was an opportunity too good to miss, so I bought some. Having no bags I put about four oranges in each of the two pockets on the front of my leather coat. That evening going through Preston Park in Brighton on my way home I was overtaken by a chap in a three wheel Morgan car, which carried its spare wheel on the back of the body. I set off to keep pace with the Morgan when it went over a bump in the road and the spare wheel, number plate and rear light fell off into the road right in front of me. I hit the wheel, flew over the handlebars and landed flat down in the road. I got up to check for injury and found a dark stain down both sides of my leather coat – I thought I had disembowelled myself and was about to die at any minute. It turned out that the oranges I had bought probably saved me from serious injury as they had been reduced to orange squash in the pockets and had leaked out down my front.

I continued to have many adventures on the bike until I went into the army in 1949 for National Service.

During this period I had a brief flirtation with another motorcycle. A school friend, Tim the younger of the two Polehill brothers who were the sons of the Vicar of Crawley, had acquired a 1920s 500cc Triumph bike which his mother would not let him keep, so he offered it to me for five pounds (quite a lot in those days). To have a big bike with chain drive, three gears and a kick start and other desirables was too good to turn down so I agreed to buy it. After school one day I went with Tim by train to Crawley to collect the bike. Crawley vicarage was a tall ugly gaunt four storey cement rendered house with a large garden divided up into beds with narrow paths between which was used by the boys' mother, a gaunt woman who matched her house, to grow tulips for sale to eke out the Vicar's modest stipend.

The motorcycle was hidden in the potting shed at the far end of the garden. Tim and I got the bike out and I was asked to go before his mother knew I was there. We started the bike, which had large running boards rather than the usual footrests, and I set off for the road along the narrow path between the beds of in-flower tulips. I

Chapter 10

lost control, jumped off the path and with Tim yelling at me to go I careered off across the soft flowerbeds rather like Boadicea's chariot – I left a deep wheel track on either side of which was a foot wide swathe of decapitated tulips. A final backwards glance revealed a contorted woman's face at an upstairs window screaming something I could not understand. The bike and I went home.

The ownership of this bike was not a success. The engine was an air cooled in line twin and had some design fault which caused the rear cylinder to overheat to the extent that after about four miles running the rear cylinder got hot enough to scorch your trouser legs. This was the signal to stop and let the engine cool down. Being impatient for this to happen naturally part of the equipment carried was a baked bean tin with a wire handle with which to scoop up water from puddles or a ditch to throw on the engine to cool it down. How this did not crack the rear cylinder I do not know.

Anyway, one fateful cold damp November day I had done about three miles and the engine got hot. I found a lay-by where the County Council kept gritty sand for treating icy roads. The bike only had a rear stand and as a very heavy bike it was difficult to get onto the stand, so if I could I would lean it on something. In this case it was a big pile of gritty sand in a bin with a back wall behind which there was a ditch with water. I leant the bike down on its left side which meant that the two Amal carburetters were uppermost and climbed over the wall to scoop water out of the ditch, pop up and throw it on the engine. This I did several times so that a cloud of steam hung over the bike. The next time I popped up there was a car stopped by the bike and a man scooping up the gritty sand and putting it on the bike. I asked him what he thought he was doing and he replied putting the fire out. I pointed out that it was steam not smoke. He said he was sorry and drove away. When I looked the whole bike engine was covered in gritty sand, particularly the carburetters whose bell mouths were pointing up and were full. I tried to clear out the carburetters with a finger and I eventually restarted the bike, but it was never the same so I sold it and returned to the Omega which I had kept.

I came home on Christmas Eve 1949 on leave from my army National Service. After the tragedy with my dog Paddy, I pulled myself together enough to get the Omega out to ride into Horsham to buy modest Christmas presents. While riding into town I found the tyres needed blowing up to the sixty psi used for beaded edged tyres. The garage I went to was Rices at the end of Albion Road where an attendant had to do everything. So I ordered petrol/oil and the tyres pumped up from a surly youth who had probably been drinking. I had the tragedy of my dog on my mind and did not supervise these activities as I should have done. The job done I rode off, up West Street in

Chapter 10

Horsham in those days. The road was crowded with shoppers and when I reached the other end there was a loud bang and the bike went out of control. I careered over the pavement, through the people, and came to rest in the glazed entrance arcade of a shop named Hunts. There was a red tongue of rubber, the remains of the inner tube, hanging out of the front tyre, which had obviously been over-inflated by the drunken youth. I had to push the bike home going slap slap and was unable to buy any Christmas presents, which did not go down well.

Sometime later I saved up and bought and fitted a new inner tube and advertised the bike for sale. I sold the bike to the two brothers Carmichael, the sons of Carmichael the head of a big London building firm who lived in Westlands Cottage in Foundry Lane after being bombed out during the War. This house I bought for my offices some twenty years later.

My school friend Richard Reed had an uncle, Henry, who had a little overgrown ramshackle car repair business near the Dog & Bacon pub, Horsham. Richard and I used to spend time with Uncle Henry and we were given an Austin 7 chassis buried in brambles. We got it going with Uncle Henry's help but it had no body. From a scrap yard we got two of the aircraft drop-tanks, like those dropped in the lagoons at Clacton mentioned in the boat section of this book, the steel teardrop shaped versions. With a jigsaw we

Cars and Bikes - Part 1

cut away part of the sides of the tanks and mounted them on either side of our chassis and filled in the 'bonnet' and 'boot' with thin steel plate and made an all enveloping bodied Austin 7 Special which was unique.

We had lots of fun with this car including a visit to the first ever International motor race meeting at Goodwood at Easter in 1949. The engine was very worn when we got the car and it gradually got worse until the car would hardly go at all. We could not afford a re-bore and so bought some Holt 'Piston Seal' which one summer evening we poured through the sparking plug holes as instructed and then went for a run down North Parade in Horsham. We got to the end of the road when there was a terrible shriek and the engine locked solid and the car slid some distance to fetch up outside the house and surgery of Dr. James who was our family doctor, so my parents got to hear about all of this. The car never ran again.

At the end of my school days I was able to get a provisional car licence with which I learnt to drive a car using a very worn out Riley Nine fabric saloon owned by a farmer's son Peter Wing whom I made a friend because of his car. This was a good car to learn on as everything was worn out so if you could control that, then every subsequent car was easy.

Then in the army during National Service I was posted to the Radar Research & Development

Chapter 10

Establishment (RRDE) at Malvern, Worcestershire where I was one of a very small group of army personnel and I lived in Geraldine Hostel which was not unlike an army camp as it consisted of a number of huts arranged on a large site, but constructed and arranged in a civilian manner to accommodate the thousand or so young civilian boffins who worked at RRDE. Geraldine Hostel had blocks of garages arranged in several courts in all probability about forty garages in total intended for the cars of the residents. However there was only one car in the place, this belonged to an older chap in his thirties whom I shared a room with briefly when I first arrived, before I wangled a single room on my own. This chap went on to head the air accident investigation unit at Farnborough.

However a lot of residents in Geraldine Hostel had motorbikes. There were those who were keen on bikes and enjoyed fiddling with them and they annexed the garages where we had an informal club workshop to mess about with our motorbikes. There was constant exchanging of bikes sometimes for cash but more often than not just to own and experience another bike. I got caught up in this and for the year or so I lived in the Hostel I probably had a dozen bikes pass through my hands. I have forgotten most of these except for a few that I do recall. One was a 350cc Cotton which was allegedly an ex-Brooklands

Cars and Bikes - Part 1

racer. This bike had a very wobbly frame but was unbelievably economical.

Another was a Matchless Silver Hawk, a 1000cc 4 cylinder bike which was rare even in those days. This was a very big and heavy bike, very ungainly and awkward to ride. In those days the crossroads in the centre of Worcester, the nearest big town to Malvern, had traffic control by a policeman on point duty positioned in the middle. The roads were surfaced by woodblocks laid with grain vertical, at that time a common feature of some old towns and cities. On one wet and drizzly Saturday afternoon I went into Worcester and approaching the central crossroads the policeman turned his back on me, that is stopping my road, so I applied the brakes although I well knew the Matchless would not stop on wet and greasy woodblocks. The bike went down on its side with me still astride and slid across the crossroads hitting the policeman behind the knees and I had a fleeting glimpse of the policeman flying backwards over me.

The bike, with the engine still running, and I ended up in the gutter on the opposite side of the road, stopped by the kerb. The bike was too heavy for me to lift on my own so I shouted at the many bystanders to help me get the bike upright so I could shut off the engine and sort out the confusion.

This done, I turned round to find the policeman, minus his helmet which was lying

Chapter 10

some distance away, bearing down on me getting his notebook out of his breast pocket and looking distinctly displeased. Thinking that attack might be the best defence I went for the policeman saying he should know better than to turn his back on a bike on wet woodblocks. Before he could respond he saw the bike I was standing beside. "That's a Matchless Silver Hawk," he said as he bent down to look closely at the bike. It turned out he was a bike enthusiast. He put his notebook away, somebody brought him his helmet and he said to me we will forget all about this if you bring that bike over to my house in Powick, a village near Worcester, on Sunday morning so that I can have a ride on it. This I did and that is how I got away with knocking down a policeman.

Another bike from Geraldine was a Special with an HRD Vincent frame with a 500cc Scott water-cooled two-stroke engine. This bike was very fast and I remember it particularly because one Saturday I used it to go from Malvern to Earls Court, London for the 1951 Motorcycle and Bicycle show with an 'informal Geraldine motor club' outing. There was a very unpopular 'nerdy' member of this group who had a Francis Barnett two stroke who came on this run and made us all stop frequently while he caught us up. After a day at this show we each made our own way back to Malvern and met up at the garages on Sunday morning to compare notes and talk about the show.

The nerdy chap showed up with huge amounts of catalogues that he had spent the previous day collecting, stuffing them into his pockets so that they had suffered some damage. He joined in the conversation telling us what gems of motorcycle information he had discovered. One of these leaflets was a Dunlop catalogue which unfortunately had the front half torn off and lost. However the chap read out from this catalogue 'for fast road and track use tyre pressures of 100 to 120 psi should be used' and that he was off to the commercial garage at the top of the road to pump his tyres up to this recommended pressure.

Off he went and we all forgot about him until about half an hour later when he came back a little the worse for wear with the wheel-less front of his bike on his shoulder towing the rear wheel behind him. It transpired that he had pumped up his front tyre to some 120 psi when it had exploded. The front wheel disintegrated, the tyre and rim went over the roof and into the garden of a two storey house adjoining the garage. This chap was all fired up to make a claim against Dunlop until we read the leaflet ourselves and found that the quoted tyre pressures related to racing bicycle tubular tyres not normal motorcycle tyres on a well based rim.

After all the exchanging of bikes at Geraldine Hostel I ended up with a very nice Royal Enfield 350cc Bullet – a good bike which I kept for some years after leaving the army.

Chapter 10

I also had a half share in a prototype 350cc overhead camshaft Triumph racing motorcycle. This came about because I had a fellow soldier friend Geoff Singer, an ex Oundle public schoolboy, who elected to live in the digs in Malvern rather than the Geraldine Hostel which reminded him too much of school. Geoff had a Francis Barnett two stroke bike and was not really into fast bikes. We together got to know a professional Triumph motorcycle works rider of Trials bikes who lived in Malvern Link, a village adjoining Malvern. This poor chap had a nasty accident in the Scottish Six Days Trials riding for Triumph when his bike fell over, he put out his right leg to try and save it and the handlebar grip went in front of his shin while the brake lever went behind his shin and through the calf muscle of his leg. A bad injury from which he had a long recovery, in fact he never walked properly again.

As an aside I believe this accident, widely reported at the time and led to the introduction of ball ends on brake and clutch levers to avoid this injury. These ball ends are still used today on Trials bikes.

While recovering he was unable to ride a motorcycle so Triumph did not employ him and as he was a contract employee he had no income other than a very early form of National Disability Benefit. He was married with two small children and needed to raise some money. He told Geoff and I that he had some very tasty motorcycle parts in his shed which he would like us to buy on the quiet.

Although we had very little money we scraped and borrowed a reasonable sum which we paid for all of this stored motorcycle stuff, but we never found out, and never asked, how it came into his possession. These parts centered around a very special one off prototype overhead camshaft 350cc racing engine for which there were two frames, one a track racing frame, the other a high ground clearance trials frame and included a lot of cycle parts, three gearboxes, wheels, tyres etc. Ownership was shared between Geoff and I with the agreement that we would assemble the bike as a racer for me to ride in the summer and use the engine in the trials frame for Geoff to ride in the winter. This was in the early part of 1951 so we assembled the bike in racing mode and with it I entered the Spring meeting at Shelsey-Walsh speed hill climb not far from Malvern where, I think for the first time, they were allowing motorcycles to enter and about ten or twelve did so. I got kitted out for this event by buying an ex-paratroop bump hat and painting over the khaki with black and white checkers and tucking my trousers into my socks.

The biggest bike was a 1000cc Vincent Sprint Special ridden by a famous sprinter George Brown.

When the event took place I frightened myself and was the slowest of the motorcycles while

Chapter 10

George Brown made fastest time of the day and I think broke the hill record held for some time by the racing driver Ken Wharton with his single seat twin rear wheeled ERA racing car. At the end of the meeting Ken Wharton was given a huge silver cup trophy as the fastest car and made a short speech in a very upper class cultured voice. The organisers had obviously not expected to give a significant award to a mere motorcyclist and George Brown got a very modest cup which I think somebody had nipped into Worcester to buy that very afternoon. George was invited to say a few words about what he thought about Shelsey-Walsh which he did. 'Too bloody dangerous' was all they got out of him.

I took away from this event the knowledge that I did not have the skill or courage to race a motorcycle. However that same year I competed on the bike at Prescott hill climb near Cheltenham and at the autumn meeting at Shelsey-Walsh. I did not shine at these meetings either. Both Geoff and I were coming to the end of our spell of National Service and Geoff decided, having witnessed my poor showing, that he did not want to do trials, so we sold the bike to one of the Geraldine bike members.

While at Malvern Capt. Thomason, my immediate superior, asked me to help him build a Frazer-Nash sports car – famous pre War make of which there still are many around and racing in the 2000s – in a lock up garage behind a small

Cars and Bikes - Part 1

repair and petrol garage located at the end of Geraldine Road where the Hostel in which I lived was situated. We worked when we could which was most evenings and on Saturday afternoons and Sundays. This lock up garage had a coin-in-the-slot metered electrical supply which the owner had adjusted to a punitive rate which we could not afford. We redressed the balance by fixing a very powerful 'magnetron' magnet from a radar set under the meter which slowed it down to the point where I do not remember ever having to put any coins in it to continue our electric supply.

We had a new chassis, restored wheels, axles, etc and originally a one and a half litre Meadows engine (standard for Frazer Nashes of that period) but Thomason came across a two litre six cylinder Blackburn engine reputedly from a Brooklands racer. This was a must have item so in it went to replace the Meadows engine. Frazer Nash are driven through sprockets by four chains (there is no conventional gearbox or back axle differential). We had a huge box of various size sprockets but did not know which ones to use, but thinking that bottom gear was probably the most important we chose the lowest ratio available. We got the car ready without an exhaust pipe for a first run at about midnight on a Saturday. The garage was surrounded by houses so we could not start the car outside with no exhaust as it would be too noisy so we returned early Sunday morning and pushed the car out into the road. Next to the

Chapter 10

garage there was a newsagent's with a queue of people in dressing gowns and slippers waiting for it to open to get their Sunday papers, as was the habit in the Midlands in the 1950s. We parted the queue and pushed the car out at an angle to the curb, of course causing quite a stir. We started the car with deafening noise, I got into the passenger seat which was not fixed down, Thomason selected first gear and let the clutch in. The car vibrated but did not move but there were screams from behind as the road surface was loose and the wheels picked up stones and grit and threw them into the queue. Eventually the wheels found solid road base and the car shot off with me tipped up in the back.

After this successful test run we decided we must get an exhaust and silencer. We went to an old craftsman at Powick, a village between Malvern and Worcester, who made a magnificent exposed six branch manifold into a three inch diameter pipe, Brooklands silencer and a terminal fishtail all in polished copper. I drove Thomason over in one of our army tilly trucks and he set off back in the 'Nash. I followed slowly in the tilly truck. About one mile down the road I found the Nash stopped at the side of the road. I stopped and with Thomason found that the new exhaust from the manifold back for about three feet was split open as if by a giant can opener. The car had set off running on only four of its six cylinders, unburnt petrol had passed into the exhaust system and ignited with a huge explosion when the engine got hot. The exhaust had to be remade by the old boy, who was not very pleased.

The only other thing I remember about the Nash was that it was the first time that I travelled at over one hundred miles per hour.

Chapter 11 - Cars and bikes – part 2

I left the army in 1951 determined to build my own sports car as soon as funds allowed. In 1953 I bought a rolling chassis of a 1929 Austin 7 (no engine, gearbox, radiator or body) at Griffins wayside garage at The Haven, Five Oaks, Rudgwick. When I got the 'log book' which gave the registration number as UC47 27 I found that the only previous owner before me had been Earl Howe – famous racing driver of the 1920s and 30s.

I got my friend Keith Gray to tow me the seven or eight miles home from The Haven with a motorcycle and me sitting on a plank tied on with string across the car's chassis. In those days there were no special tuning firms like there are now, except for one called Cambridge Engineering, who were too expensive for me. I found an engine and gearbox in a ditch and built a body for the car when money and time allowed and eventually put it on the road in 1955. I did a few mild competitions, racing under the 750 Formula, but I never did much good as I had to be careful not to break the car. Racing rules required the car to be driven to the meeting so you had problems if you broke it racing, particularly far away at Silverstone when I was living in Horsham.

Photo 11: 1929/1953 Austin Seven 750 Formula Car 1953

Some eight or nine regulars went to the meetings in the South East of England topped up by six or seven locals, so the regulars, of which I was one, all knew each other and swapped ideas and bits. At one meeting, I think at Brands Hatch, the Seven Fifty Motor Club lads were all in the same part of the paddock chatting, when an Austin 7 Special, a 750 Formula car which none of us recognised but with a chap and girl in it, came and parked at the far end of the paddock away from us. They got out of the car and sheeted it up, they were followed in a by a big Ford V8 Pilot car with a trailer and about four lads inside. In the first race that afternoon the new car went very well driven by the lad, in the second race driven

Chapter 11

by the girl, it went even better. Some of my 750 Formula chums were most upset and complained to the scrutineers that this car was not a 750 Formula car based on an Austin 7.

It turned out that the driver was Colin Chapman whom I have mentioned earlier, the girl was Hazel who became his wife. The car was Lotus No.2 and he had done clever things which were quite beyond us, like reversing the inlet and exhaust ports. But Chapman bent the rules as he would do in future, up to Formula One. He brought the car to the meeting on a trailer, offloaded it outside and drove in therefore he had 'driven to the meeting'. For the rest of that season the Lotus was far quicker than anyone else and I decided to sell my car and build to another Formula.

I advertised the car in the October 1956 Motor Sport magazine and came home from London at about 7.30pm on a dull and wet evening to find two very dodgy looking characters standing outside my parents' house. I went indoors and my mother said that the two men outside had arrived at lunchtime to look at the car, had declined to come indoors and had been standing outside in the rain ever since. Obviously very keen. I went and collected them and brought them to look at the car. They were most impressed, and I offered to take the one who wanted to buy the car for a short run which he jumped at. We went up the Comptons Lane in which I lived and knew well, at breakneck speed which impressed the customer mightily. He paid a deposit so that he could have the car's documents and get it taxed, licensed and insured, gave me his address in Mitcham, Surrey and asked me if I would deliver the car to him. I had occasionally taken my car to my office (where it caused a big fuss as in Hadens large firm mine was the only self built car) and so I agreed to drive the car to work and then drop it off at Mitcham on my way home and continue by train. I found the house which was a very small terraced cottage in a cul-de-sac side road ending with a high brick wall. I received the balance of the purchase price in very used one pound and ten shillings notes in a brown paper grocery sack. I left to walk to the nearest station and found the end of the road now had half a dozen rough looking lads standing around. I thought they were mates tipped off to mug me for the car purchase money so I made myself look as big and tough as I could and had no trouble at all.

It was a tradition amongst my chums that we went to a club car racing event at Brands Hatch each Boxing Day. We went in 1956, the year I had sold the car, and I was very pleased to see my old car entered in a 750 Formula race (the first in the afternoon). This was the old Brands Hatch circuit where shortly after the start the track went behind some trees at Druids Corner. The race started and the field went out of sight behind the trees in Druids Corner and when the rest of the

Chapter 11

field emerged my car was not among them, it had been crashed. I was livid at the thought of my car being damaged, my anger increasing throughout the five lap race. After the race the breakdown truck went out and appeared with my car on tow and the driver sitting in the back of the truck. I rushed into the paddock and when the car came in I was incandescent with rage and went for the driver who was stuck dumb by my attack. When I paused for breath he said "It's me feet, innit" I looked at his feet for the first time and not only were they long, about size thirteen, but very wide. He took his shoe and sock off and I could see his big toe was huge and the next one to it almost as big, and when he showed me his sole I could see a deep groove from between his big and next toe to his heel. He demonstrated that his big toe and next toe were prehensile, he could use them like a finger and thumb. This stopped me in my tracks and he explained that from childhood he had been a slack wire performer in a circus and had developed these feet. Austin 7s have accelerator, brake and clutch very close together and my car had a very small footwell to contain these. He explained that he could operate the pedals by turning his foot on its side for normal road driving but in the heat of his first race he had apparently pushed all the pedals together and gone off at the first corner. I said he had better sell my car and get a car with an enormous footwell.

Some years after this in the early 1960s I received a letter from Hultons Press the publishers of Eagle Comic, which was a very popular up market serious comic paper for teenagers which ran a series of articles about unusual hobbies and young people's achievements. The letter said they were preparing to publish a piece on building and racing an Austin 7 Special which had been submitted to them and they had noticed in the supporting documents that I was a previous owner and asked whether I would be prepared to look at the draft article to see if I could add anything to it. I was immensely flattered and agreed to review the draft article. It was a complete fiction – none of it was true or correct. So I notified Hultons Press. It turned out that their person dealing with it was a girl who telephoned me and said as we both worked in London we should meet for lunch to discuss the whole thing. She asked me to bring any evidence that I had built the car. We met, she was a stunningly beautiful girl and I pointed out the fabrications in the article and told her my story and showed her a few pictures I had of my building the car. She asked me if she could have the pictures but I declined to let the only copies I had out of my possession. However I did have a couple of copies of a picture taken by our local paper West Sussex County Times,of me in my parents' garage working on the car and this I gave to her. She contacted me some two weeks later to

Chapter 11

tell me that the author of the article admitted that it was a complete fiction and had withdrawn the article. She then said they still had space for an article and would I write a true one. I declined as the whole affair had turned nasty and I did not want to be involved.

Some years later Eagle Comic did publish an article about building an Austin 7 Special written about his own car by Pat Stephens who wrote a small book 'Building and Racing My 750' which he published himself. This became the founding publication of Stoneham Publishers who grew into quite a big and successful firm. Unfortunately for Eagle Comics Pat Stephens car was not the best looking, so to illustrate the piece they decided to use the local paper picture of my car which I had given them. However, the picture published, while unquestionably my car UC7427, was an artist's copy of this photograph. I contacted the Hultons Press to ask why they had used my picture in this way. The reply was that the local paper wanted too much money for them to use their photograph and as the copy drawing did not cost them anything as it had been from a published picture they did not have to attribute to anyone. Hultons Press went out of business not long after this.

I was alerted by a friend Chris Gould, who remembered the car from his early days, that the Eagle Comic article had reappeared again in the late 1990s in the magazine of the Austin 7 Clubs Association. Subsequently it was a piece in the

Automobile, monthly motoring magazine. Shortly after this I was contacted by a correspondent of Classic Car Magazine named John Pressnel claiming that he now owned my car UC7427. He had found it in a skip and was having it rebuilt as a project by students, I think, at Warwick University. He wanted to meet me to get details of the early history of the car. When telephoning to fix a meeting he said he had also been in touch with John Malyan, committee member of the Vintage Sports Car Club, VSCC, who lived in Wisborough Green near Horsham who had the original registration 'log book' for the car and some parts.

At a three way meeting at John Malyan's place it transpired that Pressnel only had the body of my car carrying the number UC4727 while the rest of what he had was not my car. John Malyan had bought my car UC4727 complete with body some years previously to restore for him and his daughter to use in VSCC events. As built by me the chassis had a welded on tubular space frame to stiffen the chassis to which the aluminium body panels were attached. This arrangement was unacceptable to the VSCC so John Malyan had the space frame and bodywork removed and had sold these to somebody in Dorking. How it ended up some years later on a derelict chassis in a skip was not clear. However the details of my car were resolved and John Pressnel said that he was to write a series of articles for Classic Car about the

Chapter 11

life of my car now that he had all the facts and would provide complimentary copies to John Malyan and myself.

I see John Malyan regularly at VSCC meetings and neither he nor I have ever seen these articles.

However, I periodically receive enquiries for details of my car, most recently from somebody in South Africa who thinks he has UC4727 and also from the Austin 7 archivist who has to get the records of UC4727 correct. I take great pride in the fact that the special car I built in 1953 should still be around and creating interest more than fifty years later.

After the Austin 7 Special I bought a 1937 Fiat 500 from a garage in Edenbridge, Kent. Driving it home at East Grinstead the driver's door, which opened backwards, blew open and dented the wing and itself, not a good start. But the Fiat was a super car. Compared with an Austin 7 it was refined and beautifully built and, once you had learnt how to drive it, it could keep up reasonable average speeds for those days. From the outset this car needed a new battery which I could never afford so I push started the car in reverse by a leg out of the driver's door which worked fine. However, the dynamo could not keep up full headlights without draining the poor battery, so I drove the car on sidelights, which led to a couple of adventures.

Coming back from an Easter dance in Cowfold in the early hours of a Sunday morning, coming up Crabtree Hill on sidelights, I hit a large badger. Very upset I stopped and walked back to find the badger very dead. I was about to put it in the ditch when I suddenly remembered that the best quality wet shaving brushes were made from badger hair, so I loaded the badger into the car. The following week I was on holiday and I spent that entire week driving around in ever increasing mileage trips trying to find somebody to buy my badger for shaving brushes. No luck, by the end of the week the badger was smelling strongly so I had to bury it in the garden.

Sometime later I was coming back to Horsham from Rudgwick in the early hours on New Year's Day on sidelights in a snow storm after dropping off my then girlfriend, Gabi, when I could not see Clemsfold roundabout and drove straight across it demolishing a big road sign which pushed the front of the car in and stopped the engine. The exposed immobile car was a bit awkward as I had no road fund licence so I pushed the car for about quarter of a mile to a little used slip road, put it in a lay by, covered it with snowy branches and walked the three miles home. I got in at 4am and had to get up for work at 6am. I telephoned my friend Ted Wilkes who agreed to tow me home that evening. It was still snowy with freezing fog and the car engine would not start so no demister. As the windscreen was iced up I could not see through it so I folded back the Cabriolet roof, sat on the top of the seatback with my head out of the

Chapter 11

top. I arrived home with the hair at the front of my head in a solid block of ice. It took over an hour with hairdryer to thaw out.

I still had the Fiat when Jane and I got married and it still had a poor battery, so Jane in all her honeymoon finery had to push the car to start us off on our honeymoon. Start as you mean to go on I say.

As a newly married man I thought a better car was warranted and being impressed with the road holding on my Fiat 500 I set about building a special. A 1937 Fiat 500 chassis, running gear, suspension, and brakes and a 950cc overhead valve BMC Morris type A engine producing a lot more power than the original 500 engine was acquired. For the body which was to be a two-seater with child seats in the back (known then as a two plus two) my friend Ted Wilkes designed a super body which I set about building in the then new fangled Glass Reinforced Plastic (GRP).

I constructed the structural tubular framework for the body from three quarter inch welded seam electrical conduit and formed the body shape by wiring expanded metal sheeting to the inside of the conduit frame and then plastering up to the level of the top of the conduit with plaster of paris faired off smooth once set. Unfortunately my sculpting skills were not up to producing some of the details that Ted Wilkes had designed but the eventual male mould was a reasonable approximation to the body he had designed.

I sealed the surface of the plaster with varnish and then polished it with Simonize, all as the current advice. As this was in the very early days of GRP the resin, catalyst and hardener were very difficult to mix properly and I obtained mine from CF Taylor at Wokingham who are mentioned in the boat chapter. Taylors also supplied chopped strand matt glass fibre which in those days had a binder which made the matt stiff so that it would not lie to curves without being cut and shut.

Then during a summer heat wave the glass fibre matt and activated resin was applied to the outside of the mould which was a difficult job as the setting time of the resin was impossible to control and a lot of the resin went off before it could be brushed out. This resulted in a very rough surface and an indeterminate laminate thickness. After the laminate had cured I set about removing the plaster moulding from the inside of the body. Theoretically the plaster sections held in by the expanded metal should have parted from the lamination without trouble. In reality the resin had penetrated the plaster making it into a marble like material which was bonded to the laminate. The only way I could get the plaster mould from the inside of the body was to chip it out with a cold chisel and club hammer. This took all my spare time for about a month.

I then had to turn my attention to the outside of the body moulding which was very rough and uneven. It turned out that the only tool that

Chapter 11

would grind off the surface was a hired industrial disc grinder, a heavy and awkward tool to use. I persisted with this for some time running up a substantial hire bill until achieving what I considered a respectable finish but which was certainly not normal car body standard. However after filling and spray painting an aluminium colour the body looked all right. The car was completed in 1963 and named FIMORAT (Fiat at either end and a bit of Morris in the middle) and it went quite well except for one fundamental fault. Intended for family use I had provided the body with a door on either side. I found that the Fiat chassis flexed so much over rough roads that the door openings visibly opened and closed, although neither door actually ever came open. So after a very successful holiday in Wales with son Nick, then about four years old and as I could not devise any way of stiffening the chassis without virtually rebuilding the car, I sold it.

While using Fimorat I had come across an MG model WA 2.5 litre sports saloon which was a pre Word War II 'super car'. This car had a very long bonnet and had been in a body shop in the Ropewalk, Littlehampton for minor paint repairs. The Ropewalk was a very narrow small road along the harbour edge which came out onto the main road through a very narrow entrance beside a cottage, the front of which was on the pavement. The owner of the body shop thought he would take the MG home for lunch without realising that the long bonnet would project out into the main road before he could see round the corner of the cottage. In the event a passing lorry hit the front of the MG and bent the entire front of the car, the wings, front axle and engine about 15 degrees out of line.

The insurance company wrote off the car and paid out the owner. The body shop owner bought the wreck and put the car in the back of his workshop with the idea of rebuilding it. When I came across it the car had been untouched for a couple of years and was covered in dust and debris. The body shop owner realised he was never going to sort the car out and agreed to sell it to me for about ten pounds. I got the car back to my parents' garage in Horsham, took everything off the front, removed the engine and gearbox and thought that straightening both sides of the massive chassis would be relatively easy. How wrong I was. Even with the help of friends and using two oxyacetylene welding torches, every jack I could borrow, pinch bars and levers and several months' weekend work I was unable to make any impression on this chassis. Eventually, in desperation, I cut through the three chassis cross members in the affected area and in one morning on my own I straightened up both sides of the chassis, welded up the cross members and achieved the desired result. I put the engine back in and straightened out and repaired everything else except for the enormously heavy gauge front

Chapter 11

wings which were beyond me so I replaced them with two strips of steel plate to get the car on the road.

The car went very well, steered and stopped just fine but was very thirsty, which was a major concern to an impecunious family man. To dispose of the MG I put an advert in Motor Sport which produced but one reply, that from a group of students at an agricultural college in Herefordshire who offered an Austin 10 in part exchange. They came with their car and were much taken with the MG. The Austin 10 was the actual 1934 motor show Austin exhibit which had been bought on a whim by a titled Herefordshire lady for use instead of her chauffeur driven Rolls Royce for shopping. Once the car was at her home she decided that she did not like it and had it properly stored by her chauffeur in one of her coach houses. The students bought it for a low but unspecified sum when the estate was auctioned on the titled lady's death. They had used it for a couple of months but it was too pedestrian for their tastes.

The exchange was completed, the students went away at high speed and I was left with a time capsule. A 1934 Austin 10 in motor show trim, as new, with only eight hundred miles on the clock. This car was interesting as on all of the cars of that period that I had owned or driven all had shortcomings which I put down to wear and old age. This car was as new but the brakes were almost ineffective, the steering was very vague, had a very rolly ride around corners and the performance was dismally poor, about forty miles per hour being the maximum speed. However, it was fairly spacious and with mats, carpets and leather upholstery it made a reasonable family car which we kept for some time. The major problem with this car was that it had no heater and was desperately cold in the winter particularly for the driver with big holes in the front of the floor for the pedals so trousers tucked into socks was the order of the day.

Throughout this period I was working in London and catching the 7:46 train from Horsham station each morning. I always had difficulty in getting up early enough in the morning to walk to the station so to speed things up I rode an old bicycle which I just dumped in the open in a yard at the station. The acid smoke from the steam trains then still at Horsham station caused the bicycle to rust away over the years until it collapsed completely. To replace it I bought and used a Vespa scooter which I managed to keep going for some time until it too succumbed to rust. I hit upon the solution to this rusting by buying a Moto Rumi Formichino (little ant) scooter which is all aluminium. This was an exotic, rare, expensive and fast twin cylinder scooter with an extraordinary performance for those days.

Chapter 11

I bought this scooter from somebody in Kilburn, North London and went by train to London on an early winter Sunday morning to collect it. This was before the days of compulsory crash helmets and I was dressed in normal clothes with a gabardine mackintosh and no hat, although I took some gloves. The controls on a Rumi are not conventionally arranged so I set off gingerly through central London traffic. I quickly found that my eyes were streaming tears with the cold wind and I was lucky enough to find a motorcycle shop in South London open on a Sunday so I could buy a pair of cheap goggles. At last I got south of the Kingston by pass and largely free of traffic and began to make faster progress. I was on a clear wide road with cars parked nose to tail on the left and with light traffic only. As I was overtaking this line of cars parked outside a church, one of them suddenly, without signalling, pulled out at right angles to cross the road and enter the house opposite. I could not stop in time, tried to steer round the back of the car but hit the rear offside corner. I flew over the handlebars of my scooter and the rear boot of the car and landed face down in the road.

I had broken my wrist and driven the goggles into the right side of my face but I was able to get up and walk. The scooter had skidded on its side to fetch up largely under one of the parked cars where it caught fire. The parked cars belonged to people who had been at the church service which

Cars and Bikes - Part 2

had just finished. They were standing three deep on the pavement and doing nothing to help. One armed I dragged the bike from the pool of burning petrol under the car, stood it upright and closed the tank filler cap which stopped the fire on the bike. The car I hit had lost its rear bumper, rear light and number plate and a lot of dried mud which was in the middle of the road.

At this point somebody shouted from the back of the crowd "I'm a doctor follow me" so I, with only one arm operational and blood pouring down my front, pushed the scooter, locked in gear, to this doctors driveway having to shout at the bystanders to part and let me through. No one gave me a hand. Righteous churchgoers went down in my estimation.

I could not push the scooter up the steep driveway slope so I leant it against the side and followed the doctor inside his house. He was angry and not very helpful, apparently because I had interrupted his lunch and I was now dripping blood on his floor. He gave me no treatment but just telephoned for an ambulance. This duly arrived shortly afterwards and after giving a statement to a policeman, who had also turned up, I was whisked off to Epsom hospital where my treatment was prompt and first class. The woman doctor made a very good job of sewing up my face. The hospital allowed me to phone Jane who duly turned up with her mother to take me home.

Chapter 11

I stayed at home on the Monday and late in the morning the doctor where I had left the damaged scooter telephoned demanding I should remove the 'unsightly' scooter from his driveway, a sympathetic gesture I thought. I contacted my friend Keith Gray and on the late Tuesday afternoon we went with his car and a trailer to pick up the scooter. While on the scene it was obvious that the car I had hit had gone up the drive and into the garage of the house opposite the doctor's house. So Keith and I went and knocked on the door of that house to make contact and discuss the accident. A middle aged woman opened the door took one look at me with bandages and an arm in a sling and slammed the door in our faces.

The police issued proceedings against the driver for dangerous driving, driving without due care and attention, failure to stop after an accident, failing to report an accident, etc, etc and said to me that these charges were serious enough for the driver to be banned and have a heavy fine.

I went as a witness to Kingston court some months later and found that the driver was the very pretty young daughter of the woman who had slammed the door. Her story was that she had recently been taught to drive by her father, who had just died. On this Sunday she had driven her mother to put flowers on father's grave. Being a nervous driver, after waiting on the left hand kerb for there to be no traffic she turned across the road into the drive without seeing me. When I hit her car she was so frightened that she had driven into her garage and shut the door and gone into her house to hide. Damning admissions I would have thought but as I said she was very pretty and the Magistrate had been leering at her throughout and handed down a punishment fine of twenty-five pounds and a licence endorsement. So much for the punishment fitting the crime.

I rebuilt the Rumi but Jane cut up rough at me driving it, so I sadly sold it without riding it again.

Chapter 12 - Cars and bikes – part 3

Jane wanted a car of her own and I bought her a Messerschmitt Three Wheeler, the rare convertible model. This was a very strange device styled as the cockpit section of a Word War II German Messerschmitt fighter plane. It had two seats one behind the other, direct handle bar steering like a motorcycle, and a 200cc Sachs 2 stroke engine which ran backwards to reverse, so you had three forward and three reverse gears. You could go as fast backwards as you could forwards, at about fifty miles per hour.

In the early 1960s I noticed in the motoring press that Fiat were replacing their post-War500 with a new model. On the off-chance I telephoned Fiat England at Wembley and asked if they had any of the replaced model 500s for disposal. They had six. I immediately went to Wembley and bought a blue Fiat 500 for £410 on the road. This turned out to be not only the first new car I had owned but one of my best buys ever. It replaced the Austin 10 and as I was then working in Brighton it became my every day Horsham to Brighton commuting car as well as a somewhat cramped but useable family transport. I loved it.

I replaced the Messerschmitt with a second hand Fiat 600 for Jane but she did not like the car so we only kept if for a short period.

Cars and Bikes - Part 3

In 1965 I started my own Practice as a Consulting Engineer and felt that a Fiat 500 was not the right image so I passed that over to Jane and bought very cheaply a MK1 2.4 Jaguar from an advert in Exchange & Mart. This turned out to be a disaster. The car was completely worn out and the front suspension gradually, over the couple of months I owned it, lowered the front of the car towards the ground. I sold this car for scrap.

I then came across an early Porsche 356 at a garage in Burgess Hill at a price I could afford, so I bought it. This was a wonderful car that I loved dearly. Although basically a Volkswagen Beetle, the Porsche modifications transformed it into a fast, comfortable, safe car which I used for business and pleasure for about eighteen months until returning from a site visit to a client college in Oxford I was hit broadside in Guildford by a van from a local motor race tuning firm driven by a mechanic who thought he was a racing driver. My insurance company wrote the car off and I bought back the wreck for twenty-five pounds. I took the car back home for rebuilding.

I needed a car while attending to the Porsche and bought a Mini Cooper 1175cc from a Horsham garage. This was an interesting and fast car. At that time Mini Coopers were successfully featuring in all forms of motor sport, however I never really liked it. I never got used to the steering position with the wheel almost horizontal

Chapter 12

and I found the car uncomfortable for any length of time. Nevertheless the Mini Cooper certainly served me well for the eighteen months or so before I finished rebuilding the Porsche, when I sold the Mini Cooper. While rebuilding the Porsche I found very serious rust in the body, which I did my best to eradicate, but as I was fully aware that this rust would break out again in the future I decided that the Porsche would not serve as a long time business transport. So a few months after completing the rebuild I sold it to the Conservative Agent for Fareham. I told him of the rust problem but he said that he could afford two new front wings so this defect did not bother him.

At about this time, many years after leaving school, by chance I came across Baldy Leppard, whom I have mentioned previously, in the George Hotel in Crawley. In the conversation which followed Baldy said his hobby was collecting ex military vehicles. I responded by saying that I knew nothing about military vehicles but that I had noticed a collection of Centurion tanks in a field adjoining the A23 at Pease Pottage, just south of Crawley.

'Oh yes," said Baldy, "they are mine." I asked what he was doing with these tanks and he told me the story.

Sometime before Baldy had wanted a tank for his collection and had gone to a big MOD auction sale of ex military hardware held up in the Midlands which catalogued a number of decommissioned tanks. When the first tank Lot came up Baldy successfully bid, I think £100. The conditions of the sale were that purchases had to be removed by the end of the day following the sale. Because of this condition there were a number of heavy transport contractors attending the sale. Baldy sought out one of these contractors who agreed to transport Baldy's tank down to Crawley. Baldy gave this chap the paperwork and payment receipt and left him to it. It was still early in the day so rather than going home Baldy went back to the sale to see what prices other things fetched. This was fortunate because shortly afterwards the transport contractor found Baldy to tell him that the Lot he had bought was for ten tanks not one, and what did he propose to do about the other nine tanks which he was not moving. Baldy had to engage virtually all the big transporters at huge expense to get the other nine tanks to Pease Pottage where he was lucky to find a friend's field in which to store them.

I said that he had pretty well got himself in a fine fix with nine scrap tanks but, "No" said Baldy. He was planning to re-commission the tanks and sell them in the Middle East. I thought this was a bit unlikely but sure enough over the next year or so the tanks at Pease Pottage disappeared one by one.

I am not sure what one can learn from this except always read a sale catalogue properly so

Chapter 12

you know what you are bidding for, and if you get it wrong hope for the luck of the devil.

Photo 12: Karmann Ghia

Enamored as I was with air-cooled Volkswagen derivatives, after the Porsche I bought an eleven month old 1972 Volkswagen Kaman Ghia convertible. This I considered to be one of the prettiest cars ever made. I used this car for some time but limited performance eventually decided me it was too nice to be left in car parks and on building sites so I put it to one side to be used only on special occasions. At the time of writing, thirty-six plus years on, I still have this car in pristine order now and with only thirty thousand miles on the clock.

Still feeling the need for a prestigious car for business I bought a Jaguar 3.4 S Automatic with sunshine roof. This was a very nice car, comfortable and fast. The children particularly liked standing on the backseat with their heads out of the open sunshine roof almost irrespective of the weather. However the petrol consumption was very high with this automatic model.

I had been in business on my own for some eight years at this time and we had never had a holiday. I was persuaded to drive to the Spanish Costa Brava on our first ever family holiday in a rented villa and I realised that the fuel costs for the Jaguar would not be acceptable. I part exchanged the Jaguar for a new Saab 95 estate car, this being chosen for seven seats and the high load potential but it was the ugliest car ever. I collected the car from the South London dealer on Saturday one week exactly before we were booked on the hovercraft to cross the Channel. On collection the dealer pointed out that the car should be gently run in and limited to 30 mph for the first 500 miles – otherwise the warranty would be voided. This was good news when I was proposing a 1000 mile high speed heavily loaded trip a week later.

Chapter 12

On the day I collected the car I awoke with a serious toothache. This persisted and got worse throughout the weekend so on the Monday I went to my dentist 'Butcher Mckee' and saw one of his partners, a young lad named Parrott. He diagnosed an impacted wisdom tooth which he said would have to be removed by a full anaesthetic operation in hospital, which he would fix up for a week or so. I pointed out that I was off on a three week holiday at the end of the week and must get something done immediately. "OK," he said, "come back at 5.30 this afternoon and I will see if I can dig it out."

I duly went back at 5.30 and came out at 8.30 with the tooth out, 14 stitches and the side of my face swollen like half a football. After the anaesthetic injection wore off at bedtime the ache returned and I did not get much sleep that night or any other night of that week. The ache gradually diminished during the following week when not only was I busy at work preparing for my holiday absence but spending the evenings driving aimlessly around the area getting some miles on the car.

Jane had asked her mother and father to come on holiday with us with the idea that they would look after the children so we could go out in the evenings. This led to Jane's mother coming up almost daily for the month before we went with some essential item gleaned from her couple of continental trips. For example, she required us to take toilet paper (because the Spaniards do not have any), candles (because the electric supply was unreliable), etc. She also demanded an anti-cholera injection before she would go. This entailed my making a special trip to Brighton to buy the vaccine and a private visit for her to my doctor to administer it.

We were booked on the 8am hovercraft from Pegwell Bay, which meant leaving home in Horsham at 6am. I wanted to load the car the evening before so the family could make this early start. To this end I asked Jane's parents to deliver their luggage to my house on Friday afternoon. When I arrived home late from work at about 7pm I found the drive blocked by suitcases left earlier by Jane's parents. I left the car outside and went in for dinner and a change of clothes. After dinner I and son, Nick, came out to load Jane's parents luggage and our own on the roof rack of the car. I went to the largest of the cases in the drive to move it to allow me to get the car in and found I could not lift it. At first I thought it was a joke, that the case was fixed to the ground, but no, it was just very heavy. It was locked so there was no way I could offload some of the contents. With some effort I could drag the case along the ground but I was definitely not strong enough to lift it on to the roof rack. This was an insoluble problem at about 9pm on a wet Friday night – until I hit on the idea of dragging the case to the up and over door of the garage, roping it to the door handle,

Chapter 12

raising the garage door, driving the car underneath and lowering the case on to the roof rack. The remainder of Jane's parents' luggage, although also strangely heavy, I could load along with our own luggage and the rubber dinghy and outboard motor which I was taking.

In the morning we were ready in good time and all got into the car. Jane's father beside me in the front, Jane, her mother and our son, Nick, behind and the two girls in the rearward facing back seats. As we set off there was a strange scraping noise, which had not been there before. I got out to investigate and found the rear wheel mud flaps, the bottom of which were normally six inches above the road, were now lying on the road, the load in the car having depressed the suspension that far. With a dull toothache and little sleep my temper was getting frayed – short of time I decided to go for it, scraping or no.

I had appointed Jane's father, a henpecked husband, to be navigator. On his lap in the car he had several books and detailed maps from the AA. I asked him to direct me to Pegwell Bay only to be told that the maps and directions were for Europe only. He had nothing for this country but he knew roughly where Pegwell Bay was.

In this manner I drove East and made reasonably good time to about Tunbridge Wells where at about 7am Jane, who had been looking at the hovercraft tickets, suddenly announced that one was required to book in at least thirty minutes before departure time. I set off flying blind at full speed to try and reach Pegwell Bay in time. The car did not like this high speed driving and developed a fault in that the engine would not run slowly, if I took my foot of the accelerator the engine died.

In the end we arrived at Pegwell Bay at about 7.45am, too late to be allowed on board. We were directed to an ancillary car park and told we would be accommodated on the next available flight.

The flight we should have been on departed and was replaced by the incoming flight which would go out again in half an hour. When this incoming flight had unloaded, the engine became covered by workmen in white overalls – obviously something was not right.

There was an AA Patrolman at the ferry terminal and while I sent the others off to get a coffee I asked the AA man to look at my car to clear the slow running jet. The man told me that he was the expert and didn't want my diagnosis of the fault and that I should go away and leave him alone. This I declined to do. He dismantled the carburetter, losing a spring clip on the throttle linkage in so doing, blew in to the carburetter body by mouth, said that he had cleared it and reassembled the whole thing and I replaced the lost linkage clip with a rearranged paper clip. When the car started it was exactly the same, the blockage had not been cleared. I said to the AA

Chapter 12

man that obviously blowing by mouth was not good enough and what was needed was a high-pressure airline which I was sure a local garage would have. Grumbling he dismantled the whole thing again and went off on his motorcycle to use a garage airline.

The only other occupants in this standby car park were an elderly couple with a motor caravan who had settled in with a table and chairs to have a picnic breakfast. During a lull in the AA man's activities I passed the time of day with this couple and asked how long they thought we would have to wait to get on a hovercraft. They replied that they went to France frequently, never booked and generally got on a ferry flight in a day or two. That did it for me, I resolved to give up and go back home when the others returned and the car was fixed. The AA man returned, reassembled the carburetter and the car was fine – except for the dodgy paper clip fixing the throttle linkage.

The rest of the family came back and just as I was about to tell them that the holiday was off and we were going home, there was an announcement over the PA system that the 8.30 hovercraft had broken down and would not be fixed for some time. Therefore there was to be a reduced one-hour service but for those who didn't want to wait a passage on the Dover ship ferry had been arranged on a first come, first served basis. Those who wanted to take advantage of this

Cars and Bikes - Part 3

offer should get their tickets endorsed by the Hovercraft office.

Naturally, there was a great rush to this office because the main car park had filled with people for the cancelled 8.30 flight and by that time also people for the 9.00 flight had arrived. I grabbed our tickets from Jane and joined the crush to get the tickets endorsed. The poor girl with the rubber stamp just couldn't cope and stamped everything presented to her without noticing that our tickets were for a flight long since gone. Due to the 'first come, first served' announcement there was a mad rush to get to Dover, so the signposted road was filled with three abreast family cars, roof racks fluttering polythene, being driven like a Grand Prix. I abandoned any caution and did quite well, being among the first to arrive at Dover. The ferry that was to take us was due to leave at 1300 hours.

We were one of the first on the Roll-On Roll-Off ship ferry and after a pleasant crossing during which we were entertained by an amateur jazz band going to some band rally in France, we were very early off the ferry in Calais. There was a Gendarme at the top of the landing ramp who stopped us and made a huge fuss about something on the roof rack. I could not understand what he was saying and my temper was rising to breaking point, but luckily another holiday maker stopped and translated that the Gendarme was worked up about my outboard

Chapter 12

motor having petrol in it – this being strictly against some rule. When I showed him that I had drained the outboard motor before we left home he grudgingly let us go. During this delay most of the cars from the ferry had gone and to try and make up lost time Jane's mother said she knew the very large Calais Docks well and would take us on a short cut to the exit. She directed us away from the signed route and I drove round sheds, between containers and over railway lines for some time. I was marvelling at how big these docks were when we came round the end of a shed to find the back of the Gendarme who had given us hassle earlier. Before he could stop us I drove round him and followed the signs to the exit which turned out to be 100 yards away. Jane's father took over the navigation now that we were in France and under his directions we set off.

We drove for about an hour straight into the setting sun – I pointed out that we were travelling West while we should be going South. This error was confirmed when we reached Caen in Brittany.

I had had enough. I had a raging toothache and a blinding headache. I left the car and went for a walk in the adjoining cornfield. On returning to the car I said I was not going any further that day and that we must find somewhere to stay the night in the next village we come to. This turned out to be a Relais Routier lorry drivers' café in a terrace of old four storey buildings. They said they could accommodate us in rooms above the café.

To access these rooms you had to go through the kitchen into what had been an inglenook fireplace and up a steel spiral staircase in the old chimney. Jane and I and our two girls were in a large room on the first floor, Jane's parents and Nick were elsewhere.

After an early night, I woke early to a beautiful sunny day. As I was lying in bed I heard a lavatory flush some way away. The sound of rushing water in the drain pipe grew louder and louder until the bidet in our room started to fill with brown liquid which rose to the rim, bobbed a couple of times then sank away taking the rushing sound with it but leaving a terrible smell behind. While I got the girls up to get out as quickly as possible several other toilets flushed in the building each time with the same result. No recommendation for French plumbing.

Feeling very much better than the evening before I worked out from a normal road map where we were and where we had to go to get back on track for Spain. Jane's mother refused to go on motorways so we then spent two increasingly hot days on Routes Nationale – old French A roads with huge camber from which the tarmac had melted to form solidified drips as ridges along the road edge over which, as a driver of a right hand drive car, I bounced for two days and some 900 miles.

The villa we had rented from a retired RAF Officer living in Sutton, Surrey was superb and

Chapter 12

the holiday village of Sagaro was fine, so from that point of view the holiday was good. The heavy suitcase turned out to be full of tinned meats, fruit and even potatoes and custard as Jane's mother would not eat "foreign muck" and had brought tinned food for the whole three weeks. Furthermore, Jane's parents did not like the sun and stayed indoors at the villa all day. They didn't come to the beach with us once. Also, they declined for various reasons to look after our children in the evening so Jane and I only went out to dinner once, and something in that meal made me violently ill.

The return from Spain went a little better than the outward journey. From recommendations by other British holidaymakers I met on the beach I determined that we would go back to Calais by motorway despite Jane's mother's protestations. To get to Avignon, to join the motorway, was about 100 miles on secondary Spanish and French roads where I was caught and fined by French motorcycle police (sunglasses and big revolvers) for overtaking a donkey and cart where there were double yellow lines on the road.

We eventually reached the motorway and set off North. Everyone was tired so it was agreed we would stop for the night at the first opportunity. This turned out to be a town called Valence on the pre-motorway main South to North road and about one mile off the motorway itself. We found a big old hotel which had the first floor projecting over the pavement to align with the road edge at the crossroads on the hill in the middle of Valence where we took rooms. Jane and I were on the first floor front corner of the building overlooking the crossroads with traffic lights. The hotel was undergoing restoration works and the kitchen and dining room were out of action. The manager recommended us to a restaurant in the small street on the other side of the town square.

Washed and brushed up we all walked over to this restaurant in the setting sun. We had a nice meal and some wine and came out into the ill-lit side street to return to the hotel after night had fallen. Ahead of us silhouetted against the brightly lit square we could see a lot of what we took to be cats in the road and on the pavement. As we got close we realized that these were not cats but enormous rats. The girls got all worked up about this but we had to run the gauntlet of these rats by walking singe file in the middle of the road with me leading the way stamping and shouting, which did not have much effect. Eventually we made it back to the hotel and gratefully headed for bed.

The weather was very hot and our room was very stuffy and airless so I opened the big tall French windows on two sides of the room to try to cool us down. This was a mistake. It was apparent that the juggernaut lorries used the old roads to avoid the motorway tolls. These lorries, with exhausts terminating vertically above the roof of their cabs at just the height of our bedroom

Chapter 12

windows, were regularly making hill starts with much engine noise, grinding of gears and copious diesel smoke as the traffic lights changed. I had to shut the windows in an attempt to keep out the smoke and noise. It then got too hot to sleep and I had to open the windows again to cool down. This cycle went on all night so I only got a total of about two hours sleep.

We set off up the motorway in the morning and made good progress, by early evening we had reached Paris. I planned to get north of Paris that evening, find somewhere to stay and next day do the short journey to the ferry port where we were booked on the 16.00 ferry. This plan, fine in theory, failed in practice due to the Paris traffic. We got completely lost and intimidated so after a couple of hours of traffic mayhem, when we had gained Northern Paris at a place called Saint Denys, we found a café with rooms over which were let out by the hour. We did a deal for the night and found clean and cheap accommodation in a brothel.

So ended our first foreign holiday – not an unqualified success, from which I returned to work more exhausted than when I left.

On return from that holiday I decided the Saab was too pedestrian for my tastes so I passed it over to Jane who used it for some years until just before Christmas one year when my car was in for service I borrowed the Saab from Jane. I started the car to be deafened by the worst engine knock I

Cars and Bikes - Part 3

had ever heard. I checked the oil dipstick, found no reading and went indoors to ask Jane when she last checked the oil. "Last Christmas" she said. She had not looked at the oil for a year. The engine was ruined and the car worn out so it was sold for scrap. For my own use I replaced the Saab with a Triumph TR6, 2.5 litre fuel injection two-seater, plus small child space, sports car. This was a very fast car which I kept for some years and enjoyed very much.

At this time Jane had bought her own car, a Volkswagen Golf GTI convertible, which was no more suitable for carrying building materials and our six dogs than my TR6. To satisfy this need I bought a new, just introduced, Suzuki FJ410. This was a very crude small off-road soft-top utility car. It was uncomfortable and slow but did the job it was bought for and I kept it for some years into my retirement.

My Consulting Engineer's Practice had been doing well and I felt a more sober image appropriate so I part-exchanged the TR6 for a new BMW 316. I loved this car which served me faithfully for several years until I went into partial retirement. As semi-retired I thought the sober image might be allowed to slip a bit so I part-exchanged the BMW for a Toyota MR2 a very fast and comfortable sports car which I enjoyed hugely until after full retirement.

Chapter 13 - Cars and bikes in retirement

Jane and I retired to West Wittering, Jane with her Golf GTI and me with my MR2 and the little Suzuki together with four German Shepherds and two other dogs. Neither of my cars suited my new lifestyle which called for a bigger utility vehicle. I disposed of the MR2 and the Suzuki and bought a new Isuzu Trooper van and had it fitted with side windows before delivery, producing an estate car version but with no rear seats.

This car served me very well for a number of years until it began to get very worn. I replaced it with a Japanese grey-import Mitsubishi Shogun with an automatic gearbox that I had been told was good for towing. Now this turned out to be untrue, when towing, the automatic gearbox with three speeds only got into top gear when going downhill, which resulted in very slow journeys. The Shogun was promptly replaced by another grey-import from the same source, but this time a Toyota Land Cruiser, a 4.2 Litre Diesel. A serious bit of motoring kit. At the time of writing I still have the Land Cruiser which is an excellent vehicle that does all I ask of it.

The steam launch Grampus which I had completed about this time, when provided with a road trailer and launching trolley, ended up as far

Cars and Bikes in Retirement

too heavy at over four tons to be towed by the Isuzu Trooper.

A lorry tractor unit was required. Initially I acquired a Steyr-Puch tractor which was a very interesting air cooled 2 stroke diesel of 14 litres capacity but proved to be absolutely worn out and the cost and difficulties in rebuilding made this idea a non-starter. I disposed of the Steyr-Puch for scrap and bought an already prepared boat transport rig from a firm of boat repairers and builders with their works inland at Curbridge while they used Hamble Yacht Services' yard on the Hamble to get boats into and out of the water. They transported boats up to forty feet long, and, they claimed, twelve tonnes in weight with a shortened chassis Ford 4D diesel arranged as a ballast tractor (like a Showman's tractor) towing a very heavy-duty trailer. They had moved their works to Hamble Yacht Services' yard and I was able to buy their transport rig.

After some overhaul work this rig was put into use to take the steam launch to the same Hamble Yacht Services for a three day Steam Boat Rally. This whole outing was a disaster. The lorry only crept along produced increasingly large amounts of smoke on the way to the Hamble until motorway traffic was slowed as by a fog. After off-loading the boat I took the lorry to a local Ford Commercial main agents geared up for emergency commercial vehicle repairs who agreed to look at it the following day, Saturday. The steam boat

Chapter 13

performed but slowly during the weekend and the lorry, although improved by cleaning the injectors, still did not have enough power to pull the boat and trailer up the sharp slope at the entrance to the marina and had to be helped by the yard tractor pulling at the front and the lorry engine at full revs. I eventually got the whole lot home and decided that I would not do that again, so I sold the Ford tractor and the big trailer and that was the last time the steam launch was in the water.

In looking for a replacement for the Ford I came across a six wheeled Range Rover Carmichael Fire Brigade Rescue Tender rated at five tonnes hitch load. Ideal. This was shortly to be offered by the Fire Brigade for disposal by tender. I asked to be included on the tender list. Three years later after I had given up on the Range Rover and solved my problems in other ways I was asked to submit a tender. I put in a ridiculously low figure, confident that I would not be successful, but in the end I was the only bidder and got the Range Rover.

This vehicle that had come from Horsham had only done some ten thousand miles in its life and had been garaged and maintained by the Fire Brigade, so I expected it to be as good as it looked. Looks can be deceptive. I received a service record with the vehicle and found that it was on its second engine and third gearbox due, I was told, to the way in which fireman drivers abused it. Furthermore, close inspection underneath revealed the under parts absolutely riddled with rust, the worst part being the two rear axle spring mounting points which were almost non existent. I went to the West Sussex Fire Brigade vehicle workshop at Tangmere to seek explanations and help. They said that standing orders at Fire Stations were that every day every vehicle was taken out of its garage and pressure washed down everywhere and then put back in its garage without being dried off, hence the rust in my Range Rover. For help they suggested a lad in the workshops called Paul James who had actually looked after my Range Rover and might do a bit of paid part-time work. Paul came to work for me part-time and became a chum. The Range Rover was eventually restored and sold on eBay for a very good price.

Notwithstanding being very much involved with boats as described elsewhere I found time to become a 'born again' motorcyclist by buying a 1977 Triumph Bonneville 750cc Special Jubilee model motorcycle with only three thousand miles on the clock. This bike was as new. In riding a bike again after a break of some fifty years I found that road and traffic conditions had changed dramatically so in order to survive I enrolled on and completed an advanced motorcycle-riding course.

I found that it was no fun going out for occasional rides on my own so I joined the VMCC (Vintage Motor Cycle Club) Goodwood section, a good crowd of mainly elderly chaps whom I get on

Chapter 13

very well with. The club organises lots of runs and events to take part in.

I then came across a partly restored 1923 Matchless R type motorcycle in Bognor which the owner wanted to sell so, to really get into Vintage machinery, I bought that. Completing the restoration of this bike has proved very difficult and it remains uncompleted. I then acquired a BMW 750cc motorcycle of the same age as the Triumph Bonneville but far superior. It was faster, handled better and was beautifully built.

I then added an interesting late 1940's Sunbeam S7 motorcycle which I considered to be the first of the super bikes now so popular. It was a very unusual immediately post-War machine which had big balloon tyres for comfort but these made cornering a very wobbly affair which I never liked.

I exchanged the Sunbeam for a car called a Robin Hood which was a Lotus Seven look alike with a tuned 1600cc cross flow Ford engine. This was a very fast car but your backside was only about four inches above the road so at traffic lights and road junctions I was dwarfed by buses and particularly lorries which, if you were on the other side from the driver, he could not see you, this unnerved me and made me feel very vulnerable.

My friend Gordon Rose who does a bit of wheeling and dealing in old cars offered me a 1933 Austin 7 Tourer which had been in a museum in Scotland. The price was right so I bought this car.

It turned out like most ex-museum cars, externally it appeared to be in good order, but mechanically it was in a very poor state. I joined the Solent Austin 7 Club and got one of their leading members David Fulton, to restore this Austin 7. He made a very good job of it and the car subsequently won a number of prizes at shows as well as being used extensively for runs and rallies.

Photo 13: 1933 Austin 7 Tourer

The next bikes I bought were first a 'basket case' Norton Dominator 88 followed by a Honda Silver Wing luxury bike both from a newspaper reporter relation of my friend John Woodhatch. The Norton

Chapter 13

I had restored by friend Ken Brady who made a superb job of it so that this bike has been my pride and joy ever since. The Honda Silver Wing luxury cruiser turned out to be a clumsy unbalanced contraption which I only kept for a short time.

While being held up from real Vintage motorcycling due to the difficulties with the Matchless, at Netley Marsh Autojumble I fell for and bought for a very good price a fully restored 1928 BSA 500 Sloper motorcycle. This is a great old bike which I have ridden a lot on runs and rallies. However it was originally designed to have a sidecar, which with advancing years I thought would be a good idea. Having been unsuccessful in finding a contemporary sidecar for the BSA Sloper I put a wanted advert in Old Bike Mart. This produced a reply from a chap in Capel-le-Ferme, near Folkestone who had several old correct period sidecar chassis for disposal. One Sunday I went to see him and bought the lot for twenty-five pounds. While there I was invited in for a cup of tea and entertained by being shown his photograph album of bikes and cars that he had owned. I was much taken with one of these, a 1905 Rexette Forecar, that is a three wheeler, two wheels at the front and one driven wheel at the back. The passenger sits on a small settee in front while the driver sits high up at the back. These cars badged 'King of Little Cars' were made with two engine sizes the more common 600cc single cylinder and the 1260cc twin cylinder of which I understand only two survive. I thought the Rexette a wonderful thing and was sorry to hear that it had been sold just a year before to a retired professional speedway rider who had hurt his leg before buying the Rexette. However I was told that this leg injury had gone bad, developed gangrene and the leg had been amputated so that this chap could not drive the Rexette which needs all your hands and feet. It turned out that the then Rexette owner was a great friend of Gordon Rose, whom I have mentioned earlier. On the following Monday morning I telephoned Gordon and asked him to enquire whether the Rexette might be for sale. He rang back later that day and said that it was and at a price less than the chap had paid for it. I bought it sight unseen. It was delivered on its own trailer to Gordon to be collected by me, so that less than seven days after seeing the photograph I was the new owner of the Rexette.

My Rexette is one of the two surviving twin cylinder models which with its 1260cc engine is really very powerful. Over the years I have done a good deal of work on the Rexette, which having 1905 technology was not very reliable, and the brakes particularly appalling. After rebuilding and trying to improve the original braking system on two occasions I gave up on that and fitted a concealed modern disc brake which makes the car useable in modern traffic conditions. With various lady passengers I have successfully completed

Chapter 13

some ten annual Pioneer Runs from Epsom Downs to Brighton for early motorcycles and three-wheelers.

Photo 14: 1905 Rexette – Jane Up

I was invited with the Rexette to one Festival of Speed at Goodwood and I did a London to Brighton veteran car run on the one year that they moved the eligible date from the usual 1904 to 1905. Furthermore, I have taken the Rexette to quite a lot of shows and rallies and picnics.

Not long after buying the Rexette, Gordon Rose telephoned to say that I had better call to see him as he had something that he thought I would want. Intrigued I went and was shown a 1920 Fiat 501S two-seat racing car. I knew I must have it. I said to Gordon that I could not buy the car because I had no money left. He said that he would be interested in doing an exchange deal. I said all I had to exchange was the Robin Hood car and the Triumph motorcycle. Much to my surprise Gordon said they'd do so I acquired the Fiat racer.

From data received with the car and from subsequent enquiries I have pieced together the story behind this car. It was delivered by Fiat to the USA in 1920 as a rolling chassis but with drawings for the two-seat racing body. The reason for this was that at that time the USA applied punitive taxes on imported cars but less or no tax on car parts. The rolling chassis was regarded as parts. I have the original Fiat drawings for the body which was put on the chassis in the USA in 1920. The car is right hand drive as at that time the races went clockwise round the circuit and as a two-seater to carry a driver and mechanic as was standard for the period.

With an engine of just under 1500cc the Fiat was built to the Voiturette Formula which had been introduced at about that time to provide cars cheaper, more practical and much safer than the Grand Prix cars which by the 1920s had become enormous engines in very light chassis and lethally dangerous. My Fiat raced in the USA throughout the 1920s allegedly by 'famous drivers'. Certainly it was raced by Elizabeth Junek a European aristocrat who was a famous and rare woman driver of the period. The car was crashed in 1929 when, with its side valve engine, it had

Chapter 13

been outclassed by the twin cam engines of later cars. My car never raced after this.

The car was 'repaired' (of which more later) and went into museums and private collections until the mid 1980s when it was in the private collection of a Robert C McLellan in Houston, Texas, having spent the War years in a mobile museum travelling the American mid-west. Englishman John Smith who had a small museum specialising, but not exclusively, in Fiats at Chudleigh in Devon in England negotiated for and bought the Fiat from Robert McLellan in January 1986. The shipment was to be by air – Houston Airport to London. On the day arranged for the flight McLellan rang Smith and said there was a snag. The US customs at Houston would not allow the Fiat to be exported. It was a protected antique and part of America's heritage. Needless to say Smith was very upset by this not least because McLellan said he had spent the money Smith had paid for the car and could not repay the purchase price. To placate Smith McLellan suggested contacting the Fiat museum people in Turin, Italy who knew all about the car and might be able to do something about the US customs.

Smith did this and was visited a couple of weeks later by a small Italian, snappily dressed in a smart dark suit with a camel coat over his shoulders and accompanied by two very large Italians also dark suited, the whole entourage like

Cars and Bikes in Retirement

the Mafia in a Hollywood film. After hearing the details of the problem the Italian told Smith that he would see what he could do to fix the difficulties. A couple of weeks later Smith received a telephone call from the Italian, then in Houston, telling him to be at London airport with his transport lorry the following day to collect the Fiat. Smith and a companion duly collected the Fiat and set off back to Devon. They had gone some hundred miles or so towards home when they were overtaken and flagged down by a police car. The policeman said you have just collected that car on your lorry from London airport. You must take it back as it has to be returned to Houston because the Americans have not granted an export license for the car. Smith told the police the whole story which won the policeman's sympathy, so he told them to carry on and he would report they had not been found.

After getting the Fiat home Smith enquired as to the circumstances that had caused London police to chase him halfway to Devon. It transpired that the Italian 'Mr Fixit' had found out that the customs staff changeover from night to day shift at Houston airport took place in the morning when the changing shifts met up in the staff canteen for refreshments together. As a result the customs barrier was unmanned for about an hour or so in the morning. During this period the car, which was impounded at the airport, was taken to a waiting Air France freight

Chapter 13

aircraft to London and then collected by Smith. It was much later that the Americans realised the car was gone and telephoned London Airport, but too late to stop Smith taking the car.

Smith's museum was in some farm buildings which he rented. The Fiat became the star exhibit in Smiths museum until 1995. In the early 1990s the farm and buildings which Smith rented had been bought by an agricultural conglomerate to become incorporated into a huge agricultural holding. Initially that did not affect Smith who had a long lease with periodic rent reviews, but in 1995 his rent came up for review and the new owners quadrupled the rent. The museum takings could not meet this increased rent so Smith closed his museum. He sold off all the cars except for his prize exhibit the Fiat racer which he took home and stored in his garage hoping to use it as the nucleus of a new museum. Time passed and by 1999 Smith realised he was never going to open another museum so he negotiated with Gordon Rose to exchange the Fiat for an antique watch which Gordon Rose had for disposal. I acquired the Fiat from Gordon Rose in January 2000 and road registered it for the first time in its life.

Ostensibly the Fiat appeared to be in good order if dirty from long storage. However when I looked into it closely it was apparent that the car needed restoration from the ground up. I was busy building my Austin 7 Special at this time so

Cars and Bikes in Retirement

passed the restoration of the Fiat over to Howard Wilson retired Chief Engineer from Beaulieu Motor Museum.

The recent publicity about my 1955 Austin 7 Special UC4727 set out in a previous chapter reawakened my interest in Austin 7 Specials and I decided to build another. There was no way I was going to the trouble of building a replica of UC4727 because nowadays things are much easier with many special parts and sports bodies available rather than having to make everything from scratch as I had to originally. I acquired a 1935 Austin 7 chassis with axles, found an engine and gearbox and sourced all of the other parts required including an aluminium Keith Roach two-seater body which, unlike GRP ones, is accepted by the Vintage Sports Car Club (VSCC). With this as a basis I started on construction of a new Special.

Howard, based in the New Forest, made a good start and stripped the Fiat 501S to its component pieces but then unfortunately died of a sudden heart attack. I had to collect up all the parts and bring them home. The only restoration completed by Howard Wilson was the cleaning and repainting of the chassis and front axle and remounting the front axle. I could not leave, for the uncertain future, boxes of nuts, bolts, small parts and parts of a car which I had not dismantled so I had to put all other projects on hold and rebuild the Fiat while I still had some

Chapter 13

memory of how it should be. I finished this car a year later, had it painted Italian racing red by my friend Graham Maguire and put it on the road, only to be disappointed by a very pedestrian performance and unpredictable steering and road holding. Further investigation revealed that while the engine was of the correct date, 1920, it was a standard engine and not the S Sports model to suit the car. Twice during the time that I was rebuilding the Fiat I had been fortunate enough to buy job lots of Fiat 501 parts which I had taken into stock for spares. Also I had become friends with Mike Crehan, a New Zealander now living in the UK, he owns and races a Fiat 501 S very similar to mine which had been built from a standard car in New Zealand and brought to the UK by Mike. He put me in touch with Alan Roberts in New Zealand who had built up Mike's racing engine and Alan agreed to build up one of my spare engines to full race specifications.

This engine rebuild took about a year during which time I investigated the Fiat chassis and found the front axle (the only part I did not restore) to be severely bent, no doubt a result of the accident in 1929 which had never been corrected as the car had not been used in anger until I put it back on the road. However I straightened out the axle and fitted period Hartford shock absorbers to both axles.

With an engine of the proper tune, a close ratio gearbox, a correct high back axle ratio and straight front axle and shock absorbers the car was transformed. It is now fast and a joy to drive and I can certainly see how it would have raced successfully in the 1920s.

Photo 15: 1920 Fiat 501S Racer

The 1920 Fiat had "Sankey" wheels with high-pressure beaded edge tyres of very narrow section. Replacement tyres are only available occasionally and are exorbitantly expensive, (at the last enquiry they were £298 each).

Later Fiats had "Sankey" well based wheel rims taking normal 'wired on' tyres. I explored every source for these well-based wheels without success but I did come across a foundry pattern for a Sankey style wheel to be cast in aluminium. I bought this foundry pattern and after modifying

Chapter 13

it for use on my Fiat I had five wheels cast up by Harling Foundry, machined by my friend Nigel Parrott, painted and then equipped with period wired-on racing tyres of a normal price and fitted to my Fiat where they looked and performed very well. I have used the car a good deal for runs, rallies and shows where it has performed well and been much admired.

I had always dreamed of owning a veteran car (that is a car built before 1 January 1905) ever since from the age of about seventeen going routinely to watch the London to Brighton veteran car run on the first Sunday in November each year and seeing the charming film, Genevieve, about the London to Brighton run made in the early 1950s. This became my mother's favourite film and it featured a continuous soundtrack of unique harmonica playing which had been composed and performed by the world-renowned virtuoso Larry Adler.

There was a side story about the film Genevieve. Just after I saw the film for the first time one of my school friends mentioned earlier, John Hempstead, came back to this country from several years in Canada where he had gone to avoid National Service. John contacted me and several other old friends in Horsham and suggested that we meet up in the Kings Head Hotel in Horsham for a drink and a chat. I and a couple of other chums met John Hempstead and went into the large lounge to sit around the inglenook fireplace for the evening. To help the conversation which was a bit stilted I was raving about the film Genevieve which I had seen only a few days previously. There was only one other person in the lounge, a little dark man sitting in the corner. Hearing my enthusiasm for the film this chap came over to us and shyly introduced himself, it was Larry Adler who was staying over night at the Kings Head. He spent the rest of the evening with us telling us how the Genevieve film was made.

With the Fiat complete I set to and finished the Austin 7 Special which had perhaps benefited

Photo 16: 1935 / 2007 Austin 7 Special

from the delay in construction because during the hiatus I managed to find a rare 1950's independent front suspension kit known as Bowden IFS which I fitted. Further I had time to

Chapter 13

fit Morris Minor hydraulic brakes to replace the notoriously poor standard Austin 7 brakes. These major items were augmented with all known minor tuning parts to create a state of the art road going Austin 7 Special.

Eventually the car was completed in 2007, painted silver, with black wings by Graham Maguire, to become a very nice, much admired, fast car which I have used for runs, rallies and shows. Whilst finishing the Austin 7 Special I went to the workshop of a friend, Ron Beasley who was a very skilled semi retired car body builder who had spent his career working with exotic cars. I got Ron to shape up the aluminium edging for the cockpit of the Austin 7 Special. Ron worked in a part of a car store behind a normal car repairs and sales garage at Lavant, near Chichester. This car store was full of desirable oldish cars among which was a chassis and engine for an early 1900s De Dion Bouton car together with the remains of a period Brougham two-seat saloon body. Ron told me it was owned by Robert King, a member of the family that owned the garage and it had been in the store for years. I asked Ron to enquire whether it might be for sale next time he saw Robert King. Sometime later Ron told me the price of the De Dion Bouton parts which was ridiculously high so I let the matter drop.

Ron Beasley must have told Robert King that I had some knowledge of Austin 7s and it appeared

Cars and Bikes in Retirement

Robert King was repairing an Austin 7 Tourer for a customer of his. Robert King telephoned me and asked if he could take details of my Austin 7 hood frame so that he could make one. He came with a chap who worked for him and immediately realised that making a replica hood frame was virtually impossible and unnecessary when I told him that such frames were readily available to buy from two or three Austin 7 restoration parts suppliers.

I next came across Robert King a couple of years later at a Veteran Car Club Christmas Party at Leonardslee near Horsham. During a conversation Robert King told me that he was under pressure from his family to clear the car store at Lavant and that the De Dion Bouton parts were now for sale at a realistic low figure which I could accept.

Due to it being squeezed in amongst a lot of other cars I had been unable to examine the De Dion closely and having got it home it became apparent that I had not bought very wisely. The chassis was of the 1904 pattern for an eight horsepower car but had been hacked about to remove a lot of the brackets and mountings required for a useable chassis. The engine was a six horse power unit of 1902-1903 manufacture for an earlier model car and the Brougham body styled and built by horse drawn carriage builders could never have been fitted to a De Dion chassis as the car controls – steering, lever, etc – were in

Chapter 13

the wrong places. Perhaps that was why the control brackets, etc had been removed in an attempt to fit the Brougham body.

Photo 17: 1904 De Dion Bouton on LBVCR

However, the most serious omission from my purchase was the combined into one unit clutches, gearbox and differential assembly which is chassis mounted at the rear, driving the wheels through universally jointed drive shafts, while the wheels are linked by a large tube independent of the chassis. This system was unique to early De Dions but so effective that this axle arrangement was used on Formula 1 Grand Prix and other racing and high performance cars until the 1960s. I had anticipated that I could find one of these gearbox rear axle assemblies without too much difficulty. This proved to be a bad mistake. I

Cars and Bikes in Retirement

enquired everywhere to be told that nobody had seen one of these units for sale for at least twenty years and I was not going to find one. I did find a firm of veteran car restorers who had made a replica gearbox fifteen years ago for a man in New Zealand and still had the foundry patterns for the casing. This gearbox cost fifteen thousand pounds originally but to produce one at the time of my enquiry would cost at least thirty thousand pounds and take a year to make.

These costs and difficulties meant that restoration of my De Dion was a non-starter. I asked my friend Gordon Rose if he could help and he said he remembered hearing some years ago about a chap in Holland who had some replica gearboxes. He would try and find out more. After some complications I was put in touch with Jaap Hoogsted in Rotterdam who had a replica gearbox. I went to Rotterdam for a few days. Jaap has been restoring De Dion Boutons for many years and has a small private museum. There he had a restored 1904 De Dion rolling chassis complete with an eight horse power engine and the original gearbox back axle assembly. After I had told him about my chassis and engine he said he would like to part exchange my De Dion parts for his restored and complete rolling chassis for the cost of the gearbox which was five thousand pounds. I jumped at this offer. I returned to Holland some weeks later with my chassis and engine and collected the replacement chassis, engine and

Chapter 13

gearbox. The only difficulty I had was on the way home. The French customs at the Channel Tunnel stopped me because they thought the De Dion parts were from some sort of gun. I was shut up in the Customs House for a couple of hours while the customs people brought in an interpreter because they could not speak English. Luckily the interpreter was an old car enthusiast who knew about De Dions and was able to sort out the customs people immediately.

I sold the Brougham body as not only did it not fit the chassis but was only a two-seater, while I wanted two rear seats to carry my grandchildren, and I set about designing a four-seat rear entrance 'tonneau' body based on pictures of De Dion Boutons in contemporary publications. This provides the driver and two tight seats in front and two small seats for children at the rear. Mark Taylor one of my ex students from sailing classes runs a Rolls Royce and Bentley restoration business in Birdham the next village to mine, and had just taken into his employ a coach builder named Ron Peachey and he was looking for work for this chap. He took on my De Dion body for cost price and turned out an excellent job. I had the body painted by another expert chum, Graham Maguire, who produced a perfect finish, and had it trimmed in brown leather by yet another chum Jerry Levers. The car was dated by the Veteran Car Club as 1904 in March 2004 with certificate no 2435. The partially completed car

Cars and Bikes in Retirement

successfully did the 2003 London to Brighton Veteran Car run and has completed every Brighton run since. Additionally this car has been used occasionally for Veteran Car Clubs runs and rallies where it has performed relatively well limited only by its age and low power.

I made two other acquisitions during the period I was doing the De Dion. I bought an unrestored rolling chassis of a 1923 Peugeot 172 BC Charrette-Normande. This is a little French car, allegedly designed by Bugatti, an example of which was acquired by Herbert Austin in the early 1920s and used for a basis of his design of the Austin 7. It was because of this that I wanted this little car and sure enough the chassis and suspension is very like an Austin 7 although very much more robust. My model, a Charrette-Normande or (Normandy cart) is a miniature pick-up truck, the back was originally zinc lined and the now only just readable sign writing proclaims it to be a 'knackers' (dead animals) truck although due to its size the only animals it could carry would be one dead sheep. I had the mechanical parts restored by Richard Peskett, a very long and expensive process, and a new replica body built by Ron Peachey the same chap who did the De Dion, using oak panelling saved from our house Westlands when we moved, and ash framing to create an exact replica of the original. At the time of writing I have not had time to finish this Peugeot car.

Chapter 13

The other purchase was a Moto Rumi Formichino scooter. I had always hankered after another Rumi to replace that which I had an accident on in the 1950s before I really got to know the bike. I came across a Rumi in poor condition but at the right price which I bought. Being very busy working on the other projects I passed the restoration of the Rumi over to Ian Skinner a member of the Rumi club which I had joined. He made a very good job of the scooter which I had painted Ferrari racing red. Unfortunately when completed and put on the road I found that my memory had played tricks on me as the performance, while probably impressive in the 1950s, was now very pedestrian and the exhaust noise, a most attractive feature of Rumis in the fifties, was now embarrassingly obtrusive for an old man. So after keeping the Rumi in store for a few years I sold it for a good price.

Working on my Fiat 501 S Racer I had been very impressed with the quality of the build of this car so when I was offered a 1926 Fiat 501 Tourer standard car in original unmolested condition I decided to buy it as a companion to the racer. This blue Tourer has all original parts, even down to the chassis number on the bonnet catches and correct headlamp glasses, and turned out to be a good buy. I have only had to have the radiator re-cored due to eighty years of blocking sediment and to replace the engine valves with less worn ones from my stocks. It is a comfortable car to drive which easily carries three adults and two children and with a new hood is and has been used in various weather conditions for many successful outings and a few rallies and shows.

Photo 18: 1926 501 Tourer

I occasionally used to make small donations to my grandchildren when they were in need of financial help. I realised the folly of doing that out of taxed income. At the same time I was conscious that my collection of cars and motorbikes was increasing in value particularly the veteran machines, and was likely to continue to do so. This brought me to consider how I could pass those items on into the family without inheritance tax and simultaneously provide my grandchildren with a regular small income to help with their education costs. A solution was to create the Groves Collection Trust 2002, The foundation of this was

Chapter 13

to make over the freehold of Number 1 Grove House, the original cottage office, to the Trust so that the rental income was to the Trust. Of course the Trust paid tax on that income but if the income was divided between and paid to my grandchildren while they had no tax liability then they could claim back the tax paid by the Trust, hence at the end of the day they would receive monies from the Trust without tax. As an adjunct to this tax arrangement I made what are known as potentially exempt transfers of all the collector's bikes and cars to the Trust. These vehicles in the Trust became a family asset in perpetuity which would appreciate in value. The arrangements were that when each grandchild was earning their own living and paying tax they should no longer need to draw money from the Trust but that money be used to run, store and maintain the vehicles for family enjoyment.

The rules for potentially exempt transfers are that they have no tax liability seven years after the transfer and tapered relief of forty percent down to zero percent should the donor die during the seven year period. By these means I hope I have created a family asset which can go on increasing in value and giving pleasure for all those interested in the foreseeable future.

THE END